YOUR NEW Kitten

WEEK-BY-WEEK
A weekly guide from birth to adulthood

SWEET WATER PRESS

SWEET WATER PRESS

Published by Sweetwater Press
Produced by Cliff Road Books

The advice offered in this book, although based on the author's experience, is not intended to be a substitute for the advice of your personal veterinarian. The author and publisher cannot be responsible for any adverse effects resulting from the use or application of the information in this book.

ISBN 1-58173-322-4

Book design by Miles Parsons
Illustrations by Tim Rocks

Printed and bound in China

www.booksamillion.com

YOUR NEW Kitten

WEEK-BY-WEEK

A weekly guide from birth to adulthood

From litter training to nutrition, everything you need to know to get started on the right foot.

Hugh Washington, D.V.M.

This book is dedicated to the glory of God, who blessed me with the opportunity, strength, and understanding to care for companion animals and their owners; my parents for their loving support toward my education and business efforts; my wife for her loving support in the operation of our hospital and family; to my son Everett and my daughter Rachel for the love they have shown during the times I have been caring for others; and to every potential new kitten owner with the prayer that they can learn from the experiences of those who have traveled this road before.

— H.W.

Table of Contents

About this Book

A young kitten learning its way around the world is one of the cutest creatures on Earth. When a kitten is just a few days old, he or she is as fragile as a lily bloom, but can rapidly grow into a mischievous clown that can give you hours of pleasure and entertainment.

If you think you just have to have one of these court jesters, you need to ask yourself a few questions. Will you be ready for the adult version of this entertainer? Will you want an exotic breed or would a rescue kitty from a humane shelter be better for your family? How do you need to prepare for your kitten? What care will she need? People say cats don't need anything from humans. This is simply not true.

Your New Kitten: Week-by-Week is designed to help you prepare for and raise your new kitten using practical information about the situations and issues you will face. Raising a kitten is not rocket science, but, as with any pet, there is a lot of responsibility involved.

Bringing a new pet into your home without the right preparation and expectations can lead to unpleasantness and even disaster. Besides, there's no reason to do so when it's relatively easy to learn everything you need to have a happy long-term experience. It's my goal in this book to share with you everything I've learned in my years of practice as a veterinarian. I will also offer recommendations on important decisions you will face as your kitten grows and develops, and personal stories about my experiences as both a vet and a cat owner.

Occasionally I will offer some strong personal opinions about professional, societal, and ethical issues in the veterinary, breeding, and animal rights fields. Above all, my goal in writing this book is to help you minimize the challenges of raising a kitten while maximizing the many benefits of forming a deep and abiding bond with a fine animal.

If there is a single word that is key to raising a happy, healthy cat, that word is patience. Cats are not small dogs and cannot be expected to learn or obey commands in the same way that dogs do. They have their own immensely curious, playful, energetic ways about them, and most kitties are also quite intelligent. That means you and your cat can learn how to live together happily ever after. The more you learn now about what to expect, the happier your ever after will be.

The week-by-week format of this book is a convenient way to conceptualize the growth of your kitten, but in most cases you will not actually have your kitten for the first six weeks. Therefore, the first six sections of the book focus on getting ready for your new family member, although I have included some highlights of kitten development too.

You will also notice that the book stops its in-depth coverage of your kitten at the six-month point and summarizes what you will need to know for the rest of the first year. This is not because your cat stops growing and developing at that point, but because a kitten requires extensive time and attention during the first six months that will not be required later. In fact, I think it's fair to say that if you spend the first six months of your cat's life working hard to establish a strong foundation for its health and happiness, the responsibilities of cat ownership will begin to seem routine.

I hope it's apparent that this book was written *for* people who love cats *by* a person who loves cats. If reading or referencing this book helps you to become a better cat owner, then I have accomplished my purpose. Enjoy!

Hugh Washington, D.V.M.

Notes:

Notes:

Week 1: Which Cat Is Right for You?

There are several factors to take into account when deciding which cat is best for you. The following should help you consider everything you need to think about before making a decision.

FACTOR #1: WHICH BREED?

If you want a specific breed of cat, you should start your research long before you actually plan to get the kitty. If you don't have a clue what kind of cat you want, start your search by visiting your local humane society or animal shelter. Do you like adult cats with long hair or short hair? Does a short-nosed cat appeal to you more or do you like a longer nose? Contact your local cat fancier club to find out when the next cat show will be. You can see many different types of cats at a show and also get a head start on finding a breeder. Shows will often have divisions for cats that represent a "collage" of the cat breeds — the cat version of a mutt, in other words. Most cats found in animal shelters are this type of mixed domestic cat rather than purebred, but they can be some of the sweetest animals you can imagine.

If you want a purebred cat, you should be prepared to spend a little more money and also be prepared to travel to get your kitten. Visit The

INDOOR OR OUTDOOR?

There is a disagreement among cat lovers, veterinarians, and breeders about whether cats should be put outside or kept in. There are arguments for both sides, but the final call will be up to you. Those who say that a cat should be let outside to play remind us that almost all cats are fascinated by the outdoors. The birds, the grass, the trees, and the small animals all have the ability to entertain the average cat for days on end. Some people think that for this reason it is cruel to keep an obviously curious animal in a house all the time. The other side of the argument, however, cites the dangers of the outside world. Some cats don't have the instincts and knowledge to survive outside. Cars, dogs, other cats, wild animals, poisons, disease, and cruel people all pose a threat to a small animal.

- Identify possible dangers to your cat.
- Decide if you're willing to risk the life of your cat to these dangers.
- Decide if your cat shows any interest in going outdoors.
- You may want to compromise by "kitty proofing" a fence around your yard or putting plants and toys on a balcony to provide your feline friend a safe place to enjoy the outdoors. And if you have a screened-in porch, just know that your kitty will want to spend most of his time there.

Cat Fanciers' Association website (www.cfa.org) for a comprehensive list of breeds and breed characteristics. A few of these are included in the chart on page 12. If you find a breed that appeals to you because of its appearance, research whether or not cats of that breed have any traits that you might find objectionable. Some breeds may be prone to a particular set of health problems, but conscientious breeders will make every attempt to eliminate these conditions from their breeding stock.

If you opt for a less refined approach to finding your kitten, you can still learn a great deal about the general temperament of the popular of breeds. For example, Asian breeds may be a bit more active or vocal than a ragdoll cat. If you want to have a more placid cat as a pet, it would be good to know that most Siamese cats tend to be more vocal and playful. With a little effort, you can avoid certain types of mixed-breed cats based on the appearance of breeds they resemble.

It has been my experience as a vet and a pet owner that feral, or wild, cats tend to be difficult as they grow into adults. This makes sense if you consider that the traits that allowed them to survive in the wild are the same as those that keep them from trusting new or uncertain situations. A feral cat will eat your food but may be extremely difficult to handle during a visit to the vet or professional groomer.

Above all, be reasonable about your ability to dedicate time to caring for your kitten.

FACTOR #2: SHORTHAIR OR LONGHAIR?

Give careful consideration to getting a longhaired-breed kitten. Unless you have the time to regularly comb the hair free of small mats and tangles, you should not choose a longhaired breed. Keep doing your homework until you find one that doesn't require as much of your time. You and your kitten will be happier.

FACTOR #3: INDOOR OR OUTDOOR?

A major decision to make before you bring your kitten home is whether or not you will allow your

COMMON BREEDS AND THEIR CHARACTERISTICS

Breed Name	Characteristics
Abyssinian	Shorthaired. Independent, talkative companions.
British	Shorthaired. Very docile and independent.
Burmese	Shorthaired. Great personality. Curious, playful, and affectionate.
Cornish Rex	Short, distinct, crimped coat. Very intelligent, and mischievous.
Devon Rex	Shorthaired. Intelligent, extroverted, affectionate cats.
Maine Coon	Longhaired. Gentle temper. Enjoys attention and affection.
Persian	Longhaired. Intelligent, playful, and compatible with other animals and children.
Ragdoll	Longhaired. An intelligent, docile, affectionate cat. Does not have instinct for preservation and must be kept inside.
Russian Blue	Shorthaired. Active, playful, docile, and affectionate.
Scottish Fold	Shorthaired. Distinctive folded ears. Very playful and affectionate.
Siamese	Shorthaired. Very social and verbally communicative. Relationship oriented.

pet to go outside. I suggest that you keep your cat indoors exclusively, if at all possible. The threats from injuries and infections when outdoors are simply too great. I find that my patients that stay outside have far more problems with fight wounds, abscesses, lethal viral infections, toxins, and trauma. I expect an outdoor cat to live about half as long as a strictly indoor cat.

However, if you have a feral kitten or one that simply goes crazy if he doesn't go outside, then you will probably have to let him go out — for your sanity and kitty's.

FACTOR #4: COST

For almost every prospective pet owner, the bite this will take from the checkbook should be a major consideration. When you pay the breeder (or dealer, or shelter) for your new kitten, your financial commitment has just begun. Food, collar, toys, and veterinary care (both routine and emergency) are just a few of the obligatory expenses of cat ownership. You may also choose to pay for professional grooming regularly.

When weighing projected costs, be sure to consider the most typical medical ailments of your kitten's breed. Your veterinarian should be happy to help you project these costs. If you haven't yet settled on a vet, there's nothing wrong with getting two or three opinions on this subject. You may also want to consider health insurance for your pet. This increasingly popular option is available in many parts of the country, and can be a great help in dealing with unforeseen medical expenses. In any case, it is best to prepare for the likely expense of owning a cat, rather than feeling forced to scrounge for funds when a medical problem arises.

WEEK 1 CHECKLIST

✓ Decide which cat is right for you.
✓ Research the characteristics of different breeds.
✓ Give careful consideration to whether you want a long hair or short hair cat.
✓ Decide if your kitten will stay inside or be permitted to go outside.
✓ Research how much your new cat will cost – not just to buy, but to own.

Kitten Development: Week 1

- Kittens' eyes and ears are closed.
- Kittens cannot regulate their body heat and must stay huddled against their littermates and their mother.
- Kittens can support their heads and begin to balance on their chests using their front legs.

Week 2: Where to Get Your Cat?

Assuming you're not looking for an especially rare or hard-to-find breed, my advice is to choose one of the following two options for finding a kitten: a reputable breeder or an animal shelter.

BREEDER

There's no grand secret to locating a good breeder in your area — it isn't rocket science, as the saying goes. A veterinarian, trusted friend, local animal organizations, a local groomer, or good old-fashioned word-of-mouth can all be reliable means of finding a breeder who will help you to get the cat you want.

Once you have identified a breeder, arrange a visit. While looking at the available kittens, you should also closely examine the behavior of the mother. Ask the breeder specific questions about behavioral or health problems the mother may have and, if possible, visit the father of the litter and ask about his background as well.

As for the kittens, examine the area where they spend the majority of their time. If this area appears unsanitary, I advise that you strongly consider terminating the visit and finding another source for your kitten. There may be legitimate reasons for temporarily unsanitary

conditions, so I don't recommend this as a litmus test of a breeder's fitness; however, such conditions can offer a hint of the breeder's concern about disease and parasite transmission. And in the event you encounter several different breeds of cats or numerous litters, be very cautious — you may have stumbled onto a cattery (a place that breeds strictly for numbers), in which case you should examine the litters and surroundings carefully.

LOCAL ANIMAL SHELTER

Many prospective cat owners decide to adopt an orphaned kitten (or a more mature cat) from their local Humane Society or other animal rescue organization. There are excellent reasons for choosing this route to cat ownership, such as helping to control animal overpopulation and providing a loving home for a cat that might otherwise never find one. All in all, a shelter is often a very good place to find a cat that will be everything you desire, and at a greatly reduced price.

At the same time, you must be cautious when considering adoption of a kitten from a shelter. For instance, with little or no knowledge of a cat's breeding and background, there is an increased likelihood of encountering physical or temperamental problems that could be incompatible with your expectations and abilities. The key to a happy adoption lies in getting as much information as possible prior to selecting your pet.

Does the staff isolate its sick animals and take other measures to prevent the spread of disease?

You should also make a point of asking about the shelter's approach to disease prevention. Does the staff isolate its sick animals and take other measures to prevent the spread of disease among its general animal population? What is the shelter's policy on euthanasia? This second question is important: As hard as it is to accept, some cats do have terminal sicknesses that pose a significant contamination threat. For this reason a strict "no euthanasia" policy is not advisable from the standpoint of general health.

Another point to bear in mind: Visiting an animal shelter can have a powerful impact on your emotions, with so many homeless cats in need of attention and affection. Particularly if children are involved in the decision, the emotion of the moment can affect your judgment about which cat might make the best companion for you and your family. Do your best to keep emotions out of the decision-making process.

TIPS FOR FINDING A CAT

When advising prospective cat owners on potential sources for finding a kitten, I also offer a few words of caution:

Look closely at the "backyard breeder"

Far too many cat owners don't take the proper precautions to prevent their new kitten, or even older cat, from becoming pregnant or impregnating a neighborhood female. Thus their little kitty starts to get "fatter," and one day they realize she is pregnant. Then, of

WHERE TO GET YOUR CAT

Breeder: A breeder is a good option if you are looking for a specific breed of cat. Research a breeder thoroughly before adopting your kitten. Asking your vet, neighbors, and local organizations can help direct you to a good breeder, but make sure to visit and inspect the conditions of the breeder before agreeing to adopt.

Shelter: Your local shelter is a wonderful place to find a loving companion in need of a home, but you should always ask a few questions before adopting a shelter cat. Be careful, too, to avoid adopting for the wrong reasons. Sympathy for the animal's situation is a noble thing, but if the cat will not fit into your lifestyle or home environment, then neither of you will be very happy.

CAUTION!

No matter where you decide to adopt your kitten, always:

- Check out their surroundings.
- Watch the behavior and demeanor of the mother for warning signs, and watch the kittens carefully as well.
- If kittens have been kept in a dirty, cramped, or otherwise unsuitable environment, then it is probably best to keep looking!
- A kitten adopted from a poor environment is more likely to have a parasitic infection, or another disease.
- Be sure and ask what vaccinations and treatments have been given to the kittens, and follow up with the veterinarian who treated the cats.

course, the family has to find a home for the babies. This is very common, and you'll see lots of ads in the paper for "free kittens" due to this. I'm not saying to avoid this situation altogether when getting a kitten, just that you should examine the surroundings and the mommy cat with a close eye. Be sure to ask the same questions of these people that you would ask a shelter or breeder. Follow up with their vet to make sure the information is accurate. Often people are in this situation because they weren't giving the mother cat the proper care in the first place.

Be careful of pet stores

I don't want to sound as if I'm issuing a blanket condemnation of pet stores, because there are some good ones out there. However, there are also some bad ones, enough of them to make me leery of recommending the pet store as a generally reliable source for a healthy kitten. Too many stores purchase their animals from breeding farms that give little or no consideration to maintaining the characteristics of the breed. All stores are not the same, but if you choose to buy a kitten from a pet store, you should take the time to find out where the animals are obtained.

As with an animal shelter, you should also ask a pet store's management about their disease prevention and treatment practices.

You should also ask a pet store's management about disease prevention.

You should ask particularly about what the store does in terms of parasite control (for a list of common parasites, see the chart on page 59). Also ask about how the store monitors its kittens for signs of respiratory disease, and the response when disease is detected. Finally, ask which veterinarian the store works with and call the vet with the same questions you asked the store.

Beware the roadside purchase

Often individuals who are looking to unload an unwanted litter of kittens will take the litter to either a roadside location or even to office buildings to find people who want to add a kitten to their family. This is one of those common-sense issues; if this was not a planned litter, how likely do you think it is that the owners have provided needed care for the mother and litters? These situations are more likely to involve diseased kittens.

Sometimes, by no fault of the owner, the kittens are found abandoned. The warning is simply to look closely for signs of respiratory disease (mucus discharge), flea infestation, or soiled

rear ends (indicates possible parasite infection). If any of these are noted, it's best to look elsewhere. No matter the situation, I recommend

you get contact information from the people you get the cat from, and also give them yours in case they discover something in the near future about the rest of the litter that you need to know.

Keep your emotions in check

We've talked about emotions in regard to adopting a cat from a shelter, but sensitivities can play a role in any cat-buying decision. Over the years, I have encountered a lot of folks who ended up with the "wrong" cat because they allowed their emotions to overrule their logic. For example, many people settle on a particular kitten out of a misplaced sense of "duty," feeling they must rescue a cat living in unhealthy circumstances. This is admirable, but a decision made on that basis usually results in unforeseen expense (and heartache) for the new owner. When a kitten and/or his littermates appear unhealthy, they often are not displaying their true behavior and temperament.

Remember that in acquiring a kitten, you are adding a new member to your family. Bringing home a sickly kitten whose personality may change dramatically as his health improves or declines can create an unfortunate situation for you and your family.

A RARE BREED

Whether for appearance, temperament, status, or simply the fun (or challenge) of owning a rare or unusual cat, some cat owners are set on finding a particular breed. This usually involves a good deal of research, which may lead to nothing but dead-ends if the breed you've selected is not available in your area.

Of course, you may find the cat you're looking for in another part of the country or the world, but getting the cat can then require influential contacts and unlimited funds. It is also likely to create any number of additional obstacles. Do you want to "select" a kitty without seeing him in person and having the opportunity to pick one with which you feel an immediate bond? How will the kitty be transported to your home? Are you acquiring the kitty from a reputable person? How do you know for certain?

Regarding the last two questions, there may be some help available to you. Most popular breeds have well-developed "communities" of owners and enthusiasts associated with them (you can probably find these on the web). These groups can be a valuable source of information about a particular breed and its peculiarities, as well as providing assistance in finding breeders with litters ready for sale.

A growing number of reputable breeders are developing their presence on the Internet, making it easier to locate specific breeds. This, however, is an appropriate place to issue a strong warning: BEWARE OF PROFITEERS! Unless you're certain of your willingness and ability to navigate this sometimes treacherous territory, it is best that you look for your new cat close to home.

KEEP A CLEAR EYE

Regardless of where you seek out your new kitty, a final piece of useful advice is to keep a "clear eye" in selecting your cat. By this I mean that the process I have outlined in this section is designed to help you make a well-informed decision about the kind of cat that fits your wants, your needs, and your lifestyle. If you have answered all of the questions I've posed thoughtfully and truthfully, your chances of finding a kitten that is right for you are excellent.

WEEK 2 CHECKLIST

- ✓ Decide where you'll get your kitten or cat.
- ✓ Look for a reputable breeder.
- ✓ Pay a visit to your local animal shelter.
- ✓ Look closely at the "backyard breeder."
- ✓ Be careful of the common pet store.
- ✓ Keep you emotions in check.
- ✓ If you want a rare breed, do some more research into whether or not you'll be able to find that breed close to your home.

Kitten Development: Week 2

- Kittens begin to open their eyes.
- The vocal range has begun to develop — kittens can "peep," as well as hiss and purr.
- Kittens can support themselves enough to crawl toward their mother or a human voice.

Week 3: Choose Your Kitten

Remember — I recommend that you get your kitten either from a reputable breeder or by adoption through your local humane society or other credible animal rescue organization. I would recommend any pet store that provides satisfactory answers to your questions.

Once you have done your homework and decided what kind of cat is right for you, it's time to go and pick out your new pet. If you followed the decision-making process outlined in Week 1 and Week 2, you know where to go to get your new family member.

Regardless of whether your kitty comes from a breeder or a shelter, you should be aware that the minimum optimal age at which a kitten should be brought into a new home is six weeks (some breeders prefer seven or eight weeks). Of course, if you adopt a cat through a shelter, it is very likely that the cat's exact age will be unknown, although the shelter's veterinarian or other professional staff should be able to give you an educated guess.

Unless you have experience with newborn kitties, caring for a cat from birth through five weeks old presents some unique challenges and difficulties that I recommend to few prospective cat owners.

PICKING YOUR CAT

If you have determined that you want to get your cat from a breeder, the breeder you have selected will let you know when he has a litter of kittens for you to choose from. I suggest that you arrange a visit after identifying a breeder; ideally, this can be any time after the litter has reached three weeks of age.

There are two primary reasons for this visit. The first reason, of course, is to actually pick your kitten. This can be a truly special moment if, like many new cat owners, you look at a litter of six or eight kittens and — zap! — make eye contact with one whose expression seems to say "Hi! I'm your cat!" Hearing stories from folks

Tips for Choosing Your Kitten

- ✓ **DO** make sure that everyone in your household is enthusiastic about owning a cat — and that no one is allergic!
- ✓ **DO** discuss with your family members the responsibilities that come with owning a cat, including litter box duties.
- ✓ **DO** be prepared for the challenges that come with ensuring your new kitten grows into a healthy, loyal, and happy companion.
- ✓ **DON'T** buy a kitten — or accept a free one — on impulse. The more research you do, the better your decision will be.
- ✓ **DON'T** base your decision completely on sympathy for a cat that needs a home. As admirable as that is, you must be sure you're getting the high cat for your and your family. Otherwise, neither you nor the cat will be very happy.

who have had this immediate sense of bonding and attachment when picking out a kitty is one of the things I enjoy most about being a veterinarian.

The second reason for an early visit to the breeder is to establish a level of comfort and trust with the person you're buying your kitten from. First and foremost, you need to know that you're dealing with a person who loves and cares for the animals in his litters.

Establishing a relationship with the breeder will enable you to become familiar with the procedures he uses in caring for his litters.

The breeder's behavior around his cats, the cats' demeanor toward him, the sanitary condition of the area where the kittens are kept — these and other signs of the quality of attention and care the breeder provides will usually be apparent.

Establishing a relationship with the breeder will enable you to become familiar with the procedures he uses in caring for his litters, and to ask some important questions about factors that can affect the health of your kitten. (See the list on page 27 for suggested questions to ask your breeder.)

In addition to asking questions of the breeder during your initial visit, you should closely observe the litter for any telltale signs of problems that should raise red flags.

If the kittens have runny eyes and/or noses, are consistently inactive, or have evidence of diarrhea on their rear ends, you should point this out to the breeder and ask what measures he is taking to have the problem evaluated and treated. Depending on his answer, you may consider choosing another breeder.

If you are satisfied with the breeder and his procedures, and if you have spotted no visible signs of problems with your kitten, its litter, or its mother, then you should talk with your veterinarian about the breeder's answers to the questions you asked. If the vet is satisfied, then all you have to do is wait a few more weeks to bring your kitten home. In the meantime, the breeder shouldn't

decision about your kitten. The key point here is that you should get as much information as possible about the current condition, and potential future health problems, of the kitten you have chosen.

mind if you want to make another visit to your cat; this will help you get better acquainted before bringing her home, and allow you to monitor her health.

If you are adopting a cat from a shelter, you should follow the process outlined above as closely as possible, with the knowledge that answers to some of the questions I've suggested simply will not be available. In any case, however, a reputable shelter will maintain health and sanitary standards that are comparable to those of a reputable breeder. As with a breeder, the shelter's answers to your questions — and your observations — should be checked out with your veterinarian before you make a final decision about your kitten.

THE SPECIAL CASE: CARING FOR AN ORPHANED NEWBORN

The earliest days and weeks of a kitten's life are generally spent with his mother. Only in cases of an orphaned kitten will significant care need to be provided. The primary concern for an orphaned kitten is keeping him warm, fed, and well hydrated, and seeing that he eliminates regularly.

The mother's normal body temperature is around 102 degrees. This does not mean that you should keep the kitten's environment at 102 degrees, because the mother's skin is not going to be that warm. Maintaining a temperature in the mid to high 90s is probably a reasonable goal. I would avoid using an electric heating pad because a kitten will usually wriggle down to the warmest location he can find. This may result in the little one being trapped next to a hot spot on

QUESTIONS FOR YOUR BREEDER

Questions you should ask (and which no reputable breeder will mind answering) include:

✓ Does the breeder perform most or all of his own veterinary treatment? If not, which veterinarian does he use? How often?

✓ Which antiparasitic compounds did he use on your kitten's litter? Why did he choose those particular treatments?

✓ How frequently does he (or his vet) conduct a comprehensive parasite examination and administer preventive antiparasitic treatment to the litter?

✓ How frequently does he breed a new litter?

✓ Has the mother cat had health problems such as allergies, ear ailments, or orthopedic conditions?

✓ What recourse will the breeder allow you if your kitten develops a parasitic disease or other contagious sickness after you have taken him home? If a serious heritable health problem is discovered? If you have a written contract with the breeder, do you have any recourse for health problems discovered after the term of the contract has expired?

✓ Would the breeder allow you to take the kitten home now, prior to his reaching six weeks of age? (If the breeder answers yes to this question, choose another breeder.)

the pad and actually getting burned, which could be fatal. Hot water bottles or socks filled with uncooked rice can be placed in the microwave and warmed to provide a safe heat source.

The best source of nutrition for a newborn is, of course, his mother's milk. The next best choice is a pre-prepared kitten milk replacement. There are several products available through your veterinarian or possibly through a pet supply store. There are homemade recipes published online, but I have found the manufactured replacement is best. Avoid using pure cow's milk to feed a kitten. The composition of cow's milk is radically different from a mother cat's milk and can cause severe diarrhea.

Generally speaking, a newborn needs to eat whenever he stirs from sleeping and will usually eat until he is satisfied. If you try to feed him a set amount and force more than the kitten willingly accepts, Mother Nature can get very upset with you. I have had several frustrated, extremely concerned, milk-covered owners pleading for help getting their kittens to drink the extra ounce of milk the book they read said the kitten had to have. Use common sense: If the kitten isn't hungry,

If a kitten less than a week old goes for more than six hours without a meal, seek professional help from a veterinarian.

don't force nourishment down his throat. If a kitten less than a week old goes for more than six hours without a meal, seek professional help from a veterinarian. Remember, however, that if the kitten isn't warm enough, the metabolism slows and the food he has consumed will not be utilized. Keeping the little tike warm cannot be overemphasized, but don't overdo it.

Also remember that the mother cats stimulate their kittens to urinate and defecate by licking the kitten's rear end. Use a warm moistened tissue, soft towel, or cotton ball to simulate this action. We have to make room for more formula to keep things moving in the right direction.

Healthcare For the Orphaned Newborn

If you do have an orphaned kitten, the three-week milestone is time for the first general deworming. I would encourage you to use your veterinarian's recommendation at this point. If you have not made a visit to your vet yet, do so now. Have him check for parasites from a stool specimen you bring with you. A fresh sample will likely need to be obtained in order to check for certain types of parasites. The importance of this step cannot be overstated. Intestinal parasites can kill a kitten before she even reaches her first vaccination visit at six weeks. If the kitten does not appear to be thriving at any point during this early development, have your veterinarian check thoroughly for parasites and give an effective general deworming agent.

Kitty Keeps on Growing

As the kitten grows, she will begin to take more interest in things besides her next meal. With greater body size and activity, the kitten will not be as dependent on a warm environment to maintain her body temperature. You will also notice that the frequency of the feedings diminishes. The eyes open at around two weeks of age, and at three weeks the ears will open. With all the new sensory stimulation, fun times are ahead for you and your new pet!

WEEK 3 CHECKLIST

- ✓ Now that you've decided where you'll get your kitty, make a visit and choose a specific cat whose personality will complement your situation.
- ✓ Establish a relationship with the breeder or shelter.
- ✓ Ask the breeder or shelter the questions on page 27, and consult with your vet about the answers.
- ✓ Try to visit your kitten several times before adopting to try to get to know him.
- ✓ If you have an orphaned kitten, your vet should do a fecal exam at three weeks.

Kitten Development: Week 3

- Kittens have nearly tripled their birth weight.
- The ear canals start to open.
- Kittens are gaining motor control. For example, they learn to swivel their ears to follow a sound.
- Kittens begin taking their first steps.

Week 4: What to Feed Your Kitten?

For the diet of your new kitten, I recommend either Hill's Science Diet, Purina Pro Plan, or Iams kitten food, although the Whiskas and Friskies brands also offer good choices. Although other diets are available, I would stay with a well-respected manufacturer that closely studies their foods in feeding trials. Also be certain to choose a food that is formulated for promoting good urinary health.

CHOOSING A FOOD

The question of dry food versus wet food really is best answered by whether or not you are willing to brush your cat's teeth regularly. If you are not comfortable doing the dental hygiene, use dry food and plan on having your vet clean the teeth regularly. If you don't mind taking up the toothbrush, then either will probably be fine.

In a litter setting, kittens usually follow their mother's example to learn how, when, and what to eat. Early on, of course, they nurse exclusively. But between nursings, they watch their mother eat her own food; soon enough, they begin to play in solid food offered to them, and eventually learn to chew and eat as Mom does. During this transitional period, their nursing gradually tapers off (and with it,

FOOD SELECTION TIPS

- Look for quality, not price!
- Ask your vet what he recommends at each stage of your kitten's development.
- Make sure the food you choose is high in protein and low in fat.
- Look for brands that conduct feeding trials rather than content analysis.

Mom's milk supply). During this time they are generally eating the same food the mother has been eating while nursing.

When you bring your new kitten home, he will possibly still be making the full transition to cat food. Your kitten will need to remain on a kitten or growth ration until he is about a year old.
In selecting a high-quality food for your kitty, bear in mind that the pet food business is just that — a business, driven by profit and not necessarily concerned with what may be best for your pet. The key point for you, the cat owner, is to know what you are buying. The best means of selecting a high-quality cat food is to choose a manufacturer that conducts feeding trials as opposed to simply offering a guaranteed analysis.

Guaranteed Analysis

The guaranteed analysis is a chart included on cat food packaging that tells you the makeup of the product. The "analysis" is only a chemical one — in other words, it tells you what your cat will be eating but not whether those contents will meet your kitty's nutritional needs.

Feeding Trials

Feeding trials provide specific nutritional information. In these trials, a population of animals is fed a specific diet for an extended period of time, with their growth, development, and performance compared to animals fed another ration. The results of such trials are the best legitimate means of determining whether a given cat food lives up to its nutritional claims and is your best "guarantee" of the product's quality and effectiveness. The cost of performing feeding trials

undoubtedly adds to the price of a particular food, but as I've already suggested, the cost is probably well worth it — and will more than pay for itself in fewer health problems for your cat and lower vet bills for you.

DO KITTENS NEED MILK?

Newborn kittens need their mother's milk, but after that kittens and cats do not need milk, especially the store-bought cow's milk that humans drink. Adult cats are quite often lactose intolerant, and milk can give them diarrhea or cause them to vomit. While your kitten will probably lap up any saucer of milk you give her, there's no reason to get her started on a bad habit now that could cause health problems later. If you must give

If you must give your cat a treat, try cream.

your cat a treat, try cream. There is less lactose in cream, and the high butterfat is actually good for kitties. A little sip of cream will satisfy your kitten more than milk, and it is better for her in the long run.

FEEDING TIME

When?

Most veterinarians and behaviorists recommend that you leave dry food out for your cat all day for several reasons. First, cats are naturally "grazers" who like to eat a lot of very small meals rather than one or two large meals. Since their bodies aren't efficient at processing stored fat, a cat who hasn't eaten for a few days can start to sustain liver damage. Constant small meals help prevent this. Some cats can also develop a "binge-and-purge" habit if they are so hungry when it comes time to eat that they "binge" on food until they throw up.

If you're feeding your kitty canned food, you should start out with four small feedings a day, moving to three feedings a day at 12 weeks, and finally, two feedings a day at six months.

What?

Always check the nutritional labels for the following necessary dietary elements: high protein, low pH, low fat, low magnesium, vitamins and minerals (such as A, B12, thiamin, niacin), taurine, and arachidonic acid. Your cat is a meat eater, and vegetarianism can harm him. You should also make sure that you are feeding your cat the correct food for his age. Kittens need the higher protein diet of a kitten food, while older cats need the supplements in senior cat food.

How Much?

The average adult cat (approximately 10 pounds) needs about 300 calories a day in order to maintain its ideal weight. Look at the calorie count on the food that you have purchased and calculate the amount of food that your cat will need. If your cat is overweight, or is on a special diet, consult your vet about the amount of food that the cat should be getting.

What Not to Feed?

Don't feed your cat dog food (lacks taurine) or table scraps. I also don't recommend canned tuna or other canned fish intended for humans. These can cause an imbalance of vitamins A, D, and E.

FOODS THAT CAN BE DANGEROUS FOR YOUR PET

Foods that are safe for humans to eat can sometimes be dangerous or even deadly for a cat. Be sure you avoid giving your kitten table scraps, keep her out of the garbage, and familiarize yourself with the everyday kinds of foods that can be harmful to her health. Some of these include:

- **Chocolate:** (and any food or drink with caffeine): Theobromine in chocolate is very toxic to both cats and dogs.
- **Grapes or raisins:** The toxicity of grapes and raisins to dogs has only recently been discovered. While no studies have been done yet, it is believed that these fruits may also affect cats adversely.
- **Onions, garlic, and related root vegetables:** Onions contain a substance (N-propyl disulphide) that destroys red blood cells in cats, causing a form of anemia called Heinz body anemia. Garlic contains a similar substance in a lesser amount.
- **Tomatoes or raw potatoes:** These foods are members of the Solanaceae family of plants, which includes the Deadly Nightshade, and contain a bitter, poisonous alkaloid called Glycoalkaloid Solanine, which can cause violent lower gastrointestinal symptoms.
- **Milk:** Although milk is not toxic to cats, many cats are lactose-intolerant, which means that the lactose in milk and milk products produces stomach upset, cramps, and gassiness.

WEEK 4 CHECKLIST

- ✓ Decide what to feed your kitten. Do your homework on the different types of food, taking a look at the results of feeding trials.
- ✓ Research how much to feed your kitten.
- ✓ Be sure you know what NOT to feed your kitten.

Kitten Development: Week 4

- Kittens have mastered walking for the most part and are working on running.
- Kittens are learning basic instinctual responses, such as arching their backs when startled.
- Meow becomes recognizable.
- Kittens begin exploring their mother's food bowl.

Notes:

Notes:

Week 5: Buy Supplies & Get Ready!

Now that you've chosen your kitty and are just waiting until you can go get her, you should use this time to get your house ready and purchase the supplies you'll need.

KITTEN-PROOF YOUR HOME

Watch Out for Poison

You may not realize that your home is full of poisonous substances that present a real danger to your kitten. Insecticides, yard-care products, paints, paint solvents, gasoline, and antifreeze can cause serious problems. Antifreeze is especially toxic because so little is required to totally shut down the kidneys. A little bit more and the nervous system is destroyed. The worst part of this toxicity is that once the symptoms begin to appear, there is little that can be done to save the kitten. If you witness your kitten drinking antifreeze, take her to your veterinarian immediately. Speed is the key in this situation. The vet will have only a small window of time to save your kitten's life.

The important thing here is to make sure all of this stuff is out of the reach of your new kitten — before she gets ill. Don't assume that poisonous lawn chemicals are safe because they are in a bag. A kitten can chew through a bag in no time and get to the chemical. Anything dangerous should be put in plastic containers with lids, such as the Rubbermaid® products you

KITTEN DANGERS

Potential Indoor Hazards

- Furniture (rocking chairs on tails)
- Electrical cords
- Christmas tree water
- Household batteries
- Small objects
- Open doors
- Open windows

Potential Poisons

- Drugs
- Plants
- Detergents and cleaning products
- Toilet bowls — do not put continuous-cleaning tablets in your tank
- Household and lawn chemicals
- Pool chemicals
- Citronella candles
- Ashtrays
- Antifreeze

can find at your local discount or home-care stores.

If your kitten has access to your carport, garage, or driveway, be sure your car isn't leaking any oil or antifreeze. If your cat walks through this liquid, it will harm her when she licks her feet to clean them. Now would be a good time to get any leaks fixed.

Keep Kitty Out of the Medicine Cabinet

Medications are another threat to your kitten. Owners will sometimes leave their own medications out where their kitten can get to them. Even if your medication is still in the bottle or package, a determined kitten can chew through it — they are very tempted to get at the noise makers inside that bottle. Put all medications in a cabinet behind closed doors.

Protect Your Plants — And Your Cat

A comprehensive discussion of the threats of poisonous plants is outside the scope of this book. However, be aware that most toxic plant exposure is non-life threatening, but you should closely monitor what plants your pet is exposed to. You can find a list of toxic plants at www.aspca.org. Another site is the Cornell University Poisonous Plants Informational Database at www.ansci.cornell.edu/plants/.

BUY SUPPLIES

In Week 1, we discussed how much a cat can cost, and by now you should have figured out that it isn't cheap. Get your checkbook ready and make a trip to your local pet supply store before you bring your kitten home. You will have a large variety of products to choose from. In some cases you will just have to pick what appeals to you the most, and in other cases, you should do a little research.

THE SHORT LIST

Supplies Needed:

- Carrying crate
- Quality cat food
- Collar
- Food bowl
- Water bowl
- Litter box, litter, slotted scoop, liners (if necessary)
- Brush, and any other grooming products necessary

You may also want:

- Leash and harness
- Scratching post
- Toys

Carrying Crate

Make sure that it will be big enough for your cat as he grows. Some of the cheaper plastic models aren't very sturdy. Make sure that it locks securely, and that your cat won't be able to unlock it.

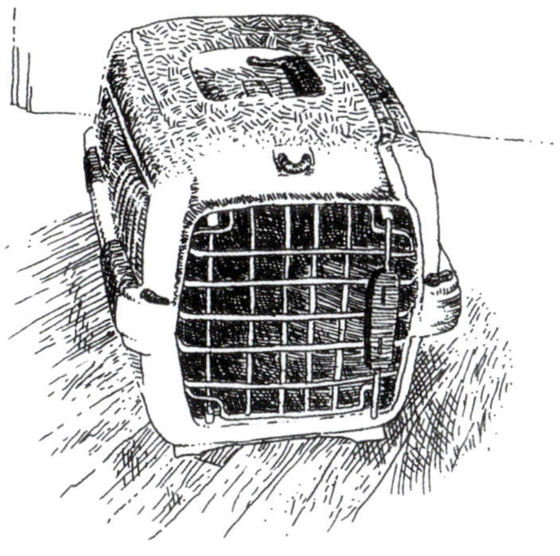

Quality Cat Food

See the chapter on Week 4 for information on selecting the right quality food for your kitten.

Collar with ID Tag

You will want the latch-release type of collar rather than a buckle collar, so your cat's collar will release if it gets caught on anything. See Week 14 for more information on collars.

Food and Water Bowls

Most pet owners find that two

LITTER BOX TIPS

DO

- Praise kitty for going in the box.
- Place the box in a quiet, safe area with low traffic.
- Keep it clean!

DON'T

- Put box in high-traffic area.
- Use strong deodorizers when cleaning.
- Put an air-freshener close to the box.
- Punish your cat for going outside the box.
- Put box in an area where he can be ambushed by another cat while in the box.
- Put box in a room with a loud noise (like a washing machine).
- Change locations or litter type suddenly.

separate bowls are more convenient than the type with two compartments. This prevents water from getting in the food and food from getting in the water. Also, if you need to wash out the food bowl, you don't have to worry about the water. Another thing to consider is that plastic bowls tend to get bacteria more quickly than metal or ceramic bowls.

Litter Box, Litter, and Liners

Do your research on what type of litter you think is best, and on the type of litter box you desire. A lidded box prevents litter from getting scattered around the outside of the box, but is harder to clean out. Do those electronic "continual cleaning" boxes work? You'll have to decide that for yourself.

Grooming Tools

You will need a comb and a brush for your cat. Most pet stores have several varieties of both. The type of brush you need will depend on whether your cat has short or long hair. Just shop around, and choose something that looks like it will work well with your cat's hair.

Toys

You should start out with at least a few toys to entertain your cat (and you in the process). Some balls and maybe a toy mouse would be a good start. See Week 9 for more information on toys.

Scratching Post

You'll see a big variety of scratching posts at the pet store. See pages 79 and 80 for more information on scratching posts.

ALL ABOUT LITTER BOXES

Litter Box Training

A common question I get is, "How do I train my kitty to go in the box?" The answer is that, in most cases, no training is needed. Cats naturally use the bathroom in a granular substance. If you have a litter box and he knows where he is, chances are he will use it with no prompting. Anyone who has a sandbox for their kids knows this is true! With young kittens, normally all that is required is buying a box

OLD CAT, NEW CAT

A lot of new kitten owners ask me how to introduce a new kitten to other cats in the house. One way is to put items that have each cat's smell on them, such as a small towel, in each cat's bed, and swap the towels out on a regular basis. This trick allows the cats to become accustomed to the scent of another cat in a non-confrontational manner.

Allowing the cats to see each other from a distance for short periods of time, possibly with one in a carrier for protection, may also be helpful. Consider using cat harnesses to allow closer contact.

Be certain to have a litter box for each cat. Having only one litter box will make things a bit close for comfort.

Pet supply manufacturers make hormonal sprays that help calm the cats and associate a more pleasant experience with seeing the newcomer in the household. Don't be discouraged if it takes a few weeks for all of your pets to get adjusted, but be warned that some personalities simply do not mix.

and putting it out. That said, there are always exceptions, and there are certain things you can do to help with the training if it doesn't happen right away.

Until your cat is completely trained, you should not leave him alone with the full run of your house. If you are leaving the cat at home, close him up in one room (with hard floors, like a kitchen or bathroom) with a bed and access to food and water on one end, and a litter box on the other. Cats naturally distance themselves from their waste, so distancing the litter box from his living area encourages him to use it.

Punishment for mistakes doesn't work with cats. Instead, when the kitten stops playing and begins to sniff or scratch, gently carry him to the litter box.

Punishment for mistakes doesn't work with cats. Instead, when the kitten stops playing and begins to sniff or scratch, gently carry him to the litter box. Give positive reinforcement, such as petting and treats, when the correct behavior is exhibited, and keep watching him.

Once a kitten has learned to use the box, avoid moving it or changing the type of litter. This may cause a relapse in his training. This is especially true as cats start to age — they like change less and less.

What Type of Litter Box Is Best?

There are many types and sizes of litter boxes available, from the basic plastic box to automated self-cleaning boxes. You may want to get one with a cover on it, or you may want to purchase liners to make cleaning easier. No matter which you choose, each cat in the house should have his own box. It's really a matter of preference on your part, because your cat will probably use what she gets used to.

Some things to keep in mind are that the sides should be low enough for your kitty to get in and out easily. If you're using a covered box, be sure that it is big enough for your cat to stand in, and to be able to turn around easily. Also be sure that it is in a well-lit area, so that it isn't too dark in the box.

Liners can make cleaning easier, but sometimes they are more trouble than they're worth. Some cats will rip them when scratching around, making the loose litter spill

Your kitten may be put off by litters that are scented. Some kittens and cats also develop allergies to scented or deodorized litter.

through the holes, causing a big mess. Then you end up having to do just as much cleaning of the litter box, if not more, than you would have done without the liner.

What Kind of Litter?

There are several different types of litter available, including the plain clay kind, the finer, clumping type, and the crystal type. Your kitten will probably use whatever you start out with, but may be put off by litters that are scented. Some kittens and cats also develop allergies to the scented or deodorized litter mixes that are popular today. Unscented litters are usually best. If you decide to change the type of litter you are using, put a box of the new litter out beside the box of old litter, or mix the old with the new, gradually increasing the amount of new litter.

How Much Litter?

The box should have enough litter in it to cover the bottom of the box thoroughly. Some cats object if there is more than about two inches of litter. Cats with long hair may be especially upset by more litter, because their hair may get in the dirty litter if their paws sink in the deep litter.

Cleaning the Box

The box should be scooped at least once a day using a slotted scooper (available at any pet or discount store) and cleaned with a mild soap and water about once a week. If you use a scoopable litter, you may be able to go two to three weeks without cleaning the box. The litmus test is whether or not you can smell the box — if you can smell it, it needs to be cleaned.

WEEK 5 CHECKLIST

✓ Kitten-proof your home by removing any poisonous substances, putting medications out of kitty's reach, and removing poisonous plants.

✓ Buy supplies for your kitten, including a crate, food, collar with ID tag, food and water bowls, litter box, litter, and scoop.

✓ Do some research on what type of litter box and litter will work best for you and your kitty.

Kitten Development: Week 5

- Kittens are able to run and play, and begin the play fighting that will teach them to hunt and protect themselves later in life.
- Social skills are being taught by the mother cat.
- Litter box training should begin around now.
- Kittens should be eating both soft kitten food and nursing.

Week 6: At Home with Your New Kitten

The day you bring a new kitten home will be an exciting day for the whole family. Now the fun begins! You are about to bring one of the most inquisitive animals alive into your home. Soon, your kitten will want to discover everything about everything.

THE RIDE HOME

If you are picking up your kitten at around six weeks of age, the trip home is usually easy. The kitten's general temperament and/or its breed characteristics will probably play a role in how active and trusting he is on the trip home. A feral kitten may cause a few problems because he wants to find a bush to hide under at all costs. A ragdoll or Maine coon kitten will likely rest calmly until he gets to the new home.

No matter how excited you are, remember that leaving his mother and littermates is a stressful time for your kitten. Your greatest responsibility at this point in your kitten's life is providing him with the comfort and security that comes with a sense of belonging to a family. Undue stress can lower the cat's resistance to infection and increase susceptibility to respiratory disease and other ailments. Stress can also contribute to an overgrowth of bacterial organisms in your kitten's system, particularly in

TIPS FOR THE FIRST DAY

- Keep your kitten close to you.
- Introduce your house to the kitten little by little, keeping her in one room for a few days until she knows her way around, then open up another room to her.
- Try to keep children and other animals calm. Their excitement may translate to fear for the kitten.
- Remind children of how fragile the tiny kitten is, and encourage them to use caution when picking her up.

the intestinal tract, which often leads to bouts of vomiting and/or diarrhea. If any of these symptoms occur during your kitten's first days at home, an immediate visit to the vet is in order.

I want to be absolutely clear on one point about stress: A certain amount of pressure and anxiety — for you and other family members, as well as the kitten — is perfectly natural, especially as you transport your kitten home and help him through the adjustment to new surroundings. In my practice, I often hear questions about ways to reduce the stress associated with picking up a new kitten, getting him home, and getting him acclimated.

Q: *Is there a best time of day or week to pick up my new kitten?*

A: Make every effort to bring your kitten into his new home at a time when you (or other members of the household) can be with him throughout his first several hours there. Be considerate of the fact that you have just removed him from the only family he has ever known, and that your kitten's every instinct says he is vulnerable. It is critical at this time that the kitten is reassured that his new family will protect and care for him, and that he will not be abandoned. Sometimes this means letting the kitten be free to explore and get used to his new home, with you close by in case he needs some reassuring. With this in mind, my recommendation is that the end of the day on the last day of your workweek is the preferred time for picking up your kitten from the breeder or shelter.

Q: *Is there a maximum distance I should travel by car to pick up my kitten?*

A: Most new cat owners get their kitten locally, but — especially in cases of rare or unusual breeds — some acquire cats from breeders in another city, state, or even country. For the sake of the kitten's comfort and health, I recommend a travel time of no more than 8-10 hours from source to home. If the driving distance is longer, you may want to consider flying. If you have to fly, check with the airline in advance to make sure you can carry your pet on board instead of checking him as baggage, which could traumatize anyone, especially a young, scared, vulnerable kitty. Note: You should check with the airline and the vet to see what paperwork will be required for your kitten to fly.

Q: *Should I take anyone with me to pick up my kitten?*

A: Assuming you are traveling by car, I recommend taking another individual along, preferably another adult or a responsible teenager. The additional person can help deal with any problems that might arise while transporting your kitten home — and help get everyone home safely by allowing the driver to keep his eyes on the road at all times.

Q: *What is the safest way to transport my kitten in the car?*

A: A small pet carrier is the best means of ensuring your pet's safety, and, potentially, your own, on a car trip of any length. A loose animal or an unsecured carrier on the seat of the car represents a serious safety hazard for the pet, the driver, and any other passengers in the vehicle, as a sudden stop can turn cat or carrier into a dangerous projectile. For maximum safety, I recommend securing the carrier on the floor of the vehicle if at all possible. I also recommend that one person be available to monitor the kitten's demeanor on the ride home, offering reassurance as necessary.

Q: *How can I keep my kitten comfortable on the ride home?*

A: With luck, your kitten will sleep for most of the ride home. I recommend as little activity as possible during this time when your kitten is beginning her adjustment to new surroundings. Have someone available to monitor her during the ride, and make sure you provide comfortable bedding in the carrier. A pillowcase stuffed with towels will make kitty more comfortable inside the carrier, and will also help contain any urination accidents that occur during the trip. The purpose of the pillowcase is to keep the kitten's claws from becoming entangled in the towel fabric. You may also want to ask the breeder for an item that may have the litter's scent on it. This could ease your kitty's feeling of loneliness for his littermates and mommy.

Q: *What about food, water, and potty breaks while driving?*

A: Food is not recommended for kittens during travel, unless you have a kitten under four weeks old, in which case you will need specialized instructions from your vet. On any trip longer than two hours, water should be offered periodically. In fact, I recommend two-hour intervals, timed around stops to see if the kitten will urinate. Have a small pan with some litter in the car for this. If your trip is of any considerable length (more than 30 minutes, say), it is probably a good idea to take along some basic cleaning materials — some liquid soap or cleaning solution and an old rag — since there is a good chance your kitten will urinate or defecate in the carrier during the drive home.

GETTING SETTLED IN

Feeding

Locate a reasonable place in your home for your kitten's food and water. Be certain that the food and water are easily accessible from your pet's primary living area, yet keep them away from major traffic areas. Otherwise, kitty can get stepped on while he is simply trying to take a drink of water.

Think Outside the (Litter) Box

The litter box should also be close to your kitten's main living area but not too close to the food and water bowls. Put kitty in the box as soon as you get home. He may just scratch around and play in it at first, but at least he'll know where it is.

Remember to clean the box daily, particularly while you are training him. Interestingly enough, a cat will still use the box even if there is just enough litter to cover the pan. Deeper levels really just help litter manufacturers sell more litter. Plan to scoop the poop several times a day, and thoroughly rinse and clean the box at least once a week.

If your kitten seems reluctant to use the box, try a variety of litter types until you find one that suits your pet. Some cats are finicky about how the litter material feels. You have to accommodate kitty — or get used to cleaning the carpet.

Boundaries

There are several training tricks that you can use to train your kitten as to which areas are off-limits. Countertops are often areas that owners wish to keep clear of cat tracks. One solution I recommend is to have a piece of stiff cardboard placed onto the counter. Have the edge of the cardboard overhang the countertop by three to four inches. You may place an empty aluminum drink can with a few coins in it on the back edge of the cardboard. This system uses the cat's tendency to land on the leading edge of a horizontal surface. Since there is not any support to the cardboard, the kitten's weight flips the piece of cardboard up from the back and sends the can into the air. By the time kitten, cardboard, and can land on the floor, the noise and uncertainty of the experience will often keep the cat off that counter.

There are mechanical devices that are essentially pressure pads that respond to the weight of the kitten and sound an alarm when there is anything on top of it. These become a bit pricey if you need to cover all your counters and tables.

THE VET'S NOTEBOOK

Up All Night in the Cat's Pajamas

Unlike dogs, cats are nocturnal animals. Even if you and your pet have a regular routine, chances are that kitty won't sleep through the night — and may not want you to, either.

When I was in veterinary school, I adopted a stray kitten who I named Sue. The youngster got plenty of playtime, but there was one game that Sue always wanted to play between 2 a.m. and 3 a.m. — "attack the feet of a sleeping man." Sue got kicked more than once just because of reflexes! She never got hurt, but she never got over her desire to play the game.

For a peaceful night's sleep, try to have a fairly active play time with your cat right before you settle down for the night. It may also help to keep the cat confined to a bed area. If a kitten doesn't have a lot of room to wander, he is much more likely to relax. Be sure he still has access to food, fresh water, and litter.

There are several herbal remedies available for calming cats. Talk to your veterinarian about this. You might also consider using Feliway® spray. A chemical copy of the pheromones present in cats, this hormone spray will cause your cat to naturally release "friendly" pheromones of his own from his facial scent glands. Spray Feliway® in doorways, on corners, and on surfaces at the height of your cat's head, and it should have a calming effect on him. Feliway® may not keep him from serenading you in the night, but it can reduce aggression, anxiety, and stressful behaviors such as spraying or clawing.

Cats with high anxiety or behavioral problems can even be prescribed the medication valium by a veterinarian. THIS DOES NOT MEAN YOU CAN GIVE VALIUM TO YOUR CAT. THE DOSAGE FOR HUMANS IS RADICALLY DIFFERENT AND COULD BE FATAL IF INGESTED BY A CAT. Medicating your cat should only be a short-term solution to a particular problem.. If your pet has ongoing behavioral problems, find an animal behavior specialist or consider finding a new home for your cat.

MULTIPLE CATS: THE FELINE HIERARCHY

Many people who adopt a cat will eventually adopt another, creating a multiple-cat home. While most cats adjust easily to a new member of the household, this situation demands a little attention from you to keep things running smoothly.

Cats naturally form a hierarchy, or chain of command, when put together. The dominant cat will accept a certain measure of responsibility for the other(s), and will demand their respect in return. Watch your cats to determine which has asserted himself as dominant.

The "top cat" will usually find the highest place in a room to rest, above the heads of the other cats, or will expect to be fed first. To avoid any territorial infringement, cooperate with the established pecking order by feeding and talking to the dominant cat first. This may seem unfair, but it will prevent any power struggles between your cats, and will make the group of them happier in the long run.

Another method for keeping cats off certain areas is to line the surface with aluminum foil. Many cats find the foil objectionable and will not tread on it.

The key idea is to create a device or system that allows the environment or the object you are trying to protect to do the punishing for you. If you rely on your correction by yelling at the cat

Another method for keeping cats off certain areas is to line the surface with aluminum foil.

to stop what she is doing, you will create a situation where the kitten only does these things when you are not present. This is generally referred to as an "owner absent" behavior. If the environment punishes for the incorrect behavior, then it makes no difference whether or not the owner is present.

Just remember that kittens do not like sudden, loud, unexpected noises or unstable surfaces. Be creative in teaching your kitten boundaries but be careful not to let

WEEK 6 CHECKLIST

- ✓ Bring your kitten home!
- ✓ Get her settled in with her food and litter box, and set boundaries for her.
- ✓ Call your vet and make her first appointment.

Kitten Development: Week 6

- Litter box training should be progressing nicely.
- Kittens begin eating dry food.
- Kittens begin to play with toys.

Week 7: The First Vet Visit

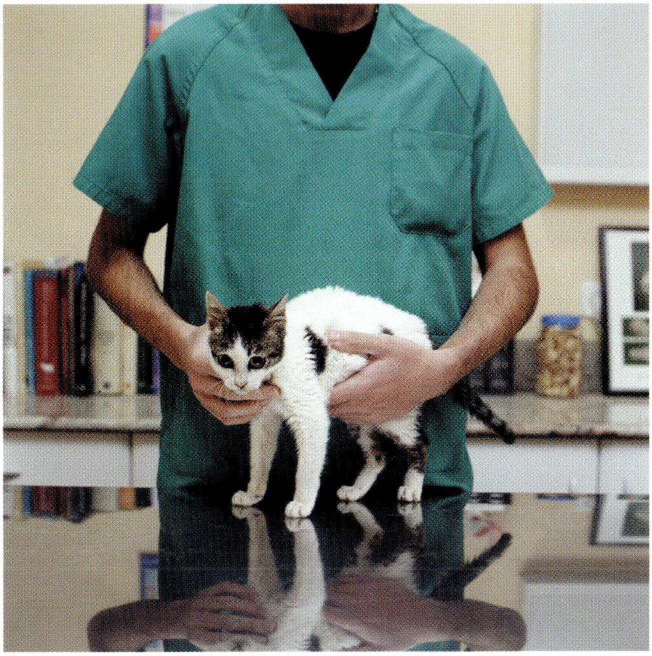

Once you have your kitten home, plan a trip to your vet as soon as possible. It should happen at six or seven weeks of age. If you have other cats at home, you may want to plan a stop at the vet on the way home. This may sound excessive, but, if by some chance your kitten is bringing a contagious virus to your home, you need to know as soon as you can. If you can't get to the vet on the way home, consider keeping your new little cat isolated from other cats in the household until you can verify that the feline leukemia virus or the feline immunodeficiency virus is not present. Either of these viruses could be devastating to other cats in the household.

If you do have other cats at home, especially outdoor cats, you may want to plan on having them tested for these viruses prior to bringing your new kitten home. It would be a shame to have your newest family member seriously ill in just a matter of a few weeks. Again, planning ahead can make a tremendous difference.

WHAT TO PLAN ON

The first trip to the vet should include another deworming (the first should have been done at three weeks), the first round of vaccinations deemed appropriate for your area, and a complete check for

Vaccination Schedule

All ages are a range. Check with your vet for his or her specific recommendations on a vaccination schedule.

3 weeks	Fecal exam & deworming
6 weeks	Fecal exam & deworming
9-10 weeks	FHV/FCV/FPV vaccine ELISA test for FeLV FeLV vaccine
12-14 weeks	FHV/FCV/FPV vaccine FeLV vaccine Rabies vaccine
16 months	FHV/FCV/FPV vaccine (repeated every three years) FeLV vaccine (repeated annually) Rabies vaccine (repeated according to local laws) Fecal exam (annually)

intestinal parasites. If you do not already have a relationship with a vet, and perhaps even if you do, ask plenty of questions about what vaccines are being given and why. There are many vaccines available

Some vets will argue that it is better to be safe than sorry and will recommend you vaccinate for everything. I would argue otherwise.

for diseases in cats, but each vaccination program needs to be tailored specifically for your situation. For example, if your cat never goes outside, never comes into contact with any cats that go outside, and has tested negative for the feline leukemia virus, then the vaccination against feline leukemia is of questionable value.

Some vets will argue that it is better to be safe than sorry and will recommend you vaccinate for everything. I would argue otherwise. Research conducted over the last ten years or so has suggested that the overuse of vaccines can actually cause harm by over-stimulating the immune system and leading to diseases of the immune system itself. On the other side of the argument, however, not vaccinating for anything will likely cause problems too. This is why you must find a veterinarian that will explain his position on vaccination to you rather than pumping your kitten full of every vaccine available. Below is a general vaccination schedule.

DISEASES AND VACCINATION

The vaccination chart includes several main diseases that your vet will likely vaccinate for. While your vet will be best equipped to help you tailor your vaccination program to your cat's situation, I'll go ahead and explain these diseases, since they are the major health threats to your cat.

FHV: Feline Herpes Virus. Formerly known as Feline Rhinotracheitis. This is an upper respiratory disease that causes sneezing, runny eyes and nose, lesions, and coughing.

FCV: Feline Calicivirus. This is also a respiratory disease with similar symptoms to Feline Herpes Virus. These two viruses account for about 95% of respiratory disease in cats.

FPV: Feline Panleukemia Virus. Also known as "feline distemper," this causes vomiting, diarrhea, fever, loss of appetite, and sudden death in cats. It is usually recognized by a yellow fluid discharge from the eyes.

FeLV: Feline Leukemia. This is the most common viral infection in cats. It can be contracted at birth from an infected mother, or through a bite or contact with the urine of an infected cat. With symptoms that vary from an elevated temperature to certain forms of cancer, this disease is hard to diagnose. Your vet can perform a blood test that is fairly accurate in diagnosing this incurable disease, but its results are not 100%. Your best protection for your cat is the leukemia vaccine, which is begun at 9 weeks and repeated annually throughout life.

An infected cat can give rabies to a human just as an infected dog can.

Rabies. This well-known disease presents similar symptoms in any species, and is highly dangerous because of its inter-species transmission. An infected cat can give rabies to a human just as an infected dog can.

Most areas require your pets to be vaccinated for rabies on either an

FELINE ASTHMA

A fairly common problem seen in cats is asthma. Many pollutants in the air can lead to problems in the lungs. Probably the most common is cigarette smoke, but seemingly innocuous agents such as perfumes, air fresheners, and carpet deodorizers can lead to significant breathing difficulty in your cat. If you see that your cat is coughing, breathing through her mouth regularly, or making wheezing sounds as she breathes, visit your vet immediately. Be forewarned that you may have to make some lifestyle changes if asthma is the diagnosis.

annual or once-every-three-years basis, beginning at about three months. A tag should be worn on your cat's collar providing proof that the vaccine is up to date. In most places, the rabies vaccine is the only vaccination required by law. This is to protect the general public from the disease.

By vaccinating your pet, you are protecting yourself, your family, friends and neighbors, and all of your fellow citizens against the possibility of contracting rabies.

Other Vaccinations to Ask Your Vet About

FIV: Feline Immunodeficiency Virus. This is similar to a feline version of HIV, but transmitted through a bite. Thus the incidence of the disease is not high for indoor cats. Any outdoor cat, however, should be vaccinated for FIV. The vaccine is available at most veterinary offices.

FIP: Feline Infectious Peritonitis. This is a controversial topic. While the disease is serious and almost always fatal, many vets insist that there is not a high enough infection rate in the cat population to justify giving the vaccine. Talk with your vet about the risk of infection in your area.

Feline Bordetella. Bordetella is a bacterial organism that infects the upper airways and the trachea. It is easily spread from other sneezing or coughing cats and is commonly spread in humane shelters, pet stores, grooming facilities, and boarding facilities. There is a three- to five-day incubation period where the cat is ill but not showing significant symptoms. Vaccination

Bordetella is commonly spread in humane shelters, pet stores, grooming facilities, and boarding facilities.

against this organism is available and is recommended if your cat will be visiting any of these facilities.

COMMON PARASITIC DISEASES

It is estimated that up to 45% of cats are infected with some sort of gastrointestinal parasite. These parasites can range from long, thin whipworms to single-celled organisms. The symptoms of an intestinal infection include vomiting, diarrhea, loss of appetite, a pot-bellied appearance, lethargy, and a dullness of the coat. These parasites feed off the cat, making her weak and lowering her immunity to other diseases.

The potential for disease transmission, specifically parasite infections, is a serious concern for all cat owners. Most owners are particularly concerned about the transmission of these infections to the children in the household. If the kitten has parasites there is a strong chance the child will become infected if he plays in the litter box. The problem is that a litter box accessible to the kitten is usually also accessible to the children in the household. This is a situation in which you might consider a covered litter box. Personally, I think that you can avoid serious problems as long as you closely watch the child — and your new pet.

Common Parasites

Roundworm	The most common intestinal parasite, caused by the ingestion of infected prey, or in humans by contact with infected feces.
Hookworm	Between 10% and 60% of cats are estimated to have a hookworm infection. They are either ingested or pierce the skin, then migrate to the lungs and then intestines.
Tapeworm	This infection is easiest to spot since the small worm segments are visible in the feces or around the cat's rectum. They look like a small grain of rice, and announce the presence of fully mature tapeworms in the cat's intestine
Coccidia	A microscopic parasite that is ingested and hatches to live in the intestine. Most cats will be infected at some point, and the infection isn't generally harmful to an adult cat, but is dangerous in kittens. Not transferable to humans.
Giardia	Also a microbial infection of the intestines, it is most common in multiple cat households. Usually transferred by ingestion from a littermate or another cat in close contact. Usually contracted by cats less than a year old. Causes severe diarrhea.
Toxoplasma	With a high rate of infection, this is one of the most common parasitic infections in cats. Actual disease caused by the parasite is not common, but the cat remains contagious to other cats.

KITTY'S FIRST VET VISIT AT A GLANCE

- Fecal examination for intestinal parasites.
- Second deworming treatment.
- Discuss vaccination options and requirements with your vet.
- Decide on a vaccine regimen that your kitten will receive.
- Discuss and decide on a heartworm preventive regimen for your cat.
- Full checkup to be sure that your kitten is free of disease, abnormalities, or other conditions that may need attention.

OTHER PARASITES

Heartworms

Heartworms in your kitten are another critical concern to address with your vet. They are infectious parasites that come from microscopic larvae carried by mosquitoes.

Heartworm disease in cats is a threat that many cat owners are not aware of. Cats with heartworm disease do not have the same symptoms nor are they treated in the same manner as dogs. The difference in cats is that the cat's immune system will react to the presence of the protein from the parasite in the body. Cats can have serious problems with either the larval stages or the adult stages of the parasite. The immature stages of the heartworm are carried by the mosquito (usually after biting an infected dog) and transferred to the cat when it bites the cat. In adulthood, these larvae will migrate through the body toward the cat's lungs and heart towards adulthood. This causes an inflammatory reaction in the cat's immune system. This reaction appears to be worse in the lungs and can lead to coughing, decreased activity, and decreased appetite.

If the reaction is to the immature stages of the parasite, the symptoms are usually minor and can be self-limiting, although some treatment is often necessary. If the cat's immune system does not destroy the larvae before they become adult heartworms, then the real problems begin. When the adult heartworm dies in the cat, there is roughly a 50 percent chance of the cat dying due to severe reaction in the lungs. This occurs regardless of whether the worm dies from old age or due to treatment by a vet.

The good news is that heartworm disease is relatively easy to prevent. The incidence of heartworms in cats generally parallels the level in the dog population in the immediate area. Preventive medications are widely available and there are regions where the disease is not a problem — specifically climates where there aren't many dogs or no mosquitoes to spread the disease from the dogs.

Do not assume that because your cat is inside that he cannot be exposed to mosquitoes. Mosquitoes come inside all the time when we open our doors at night. All it takes for your cat to have significant problems is infection from one bite from one infected mosquito. Discuss this disease carefully with your vet and plan on providing the extra care if needed.

Ringworm

A vaccine for ringworm has just come on the market in some areas. It is said to be good for both treatment and prevention of ringworm. It may or may not yet be available in your area, and since it is very new, there is not much data on its effectiveness. You may want to ask your vet about it if ringworm is a problem in your area.

FINAL NOTE

While I talk a lot about vaccinations and parasites in this chapter, the most important part of the first vet visit is the actual exam. There is no replacement for a one-on-one complete examination of your kitten by a veterinarian.

WEEK 7 CHECKLIST

- ✓ Take your kitty for her first vet visit.
- ✓ Your vet should do a fecal exam.
- ✓ Go over your kitty's vaccination schedule with your vet.
- ✓ Do some research on common diseases and parasites.

Kitten Development: Week 7

- Kittens will consistently head for the litter box, and if it's close enough they usually make it.
- Kittens still nurse occasionally if still with Mom, but should be getting most of their nutrition from kitten food.
- Kittens learn social skills from the rest of the litter and mother.

Week 8: Grooming & Pest Prevention

Grooming your cat serves several functions, including keeping her free of mats, helping to reduce skin disorders, and keeping her free of pests. This will not only make your kitten look and feel better, but is important to her overall health and well-being.

GROOMING

Whether or not you decide to take your cat to a professional groomer, you should start doing some basic grooming at home as early as possible. The younger the kitten is when you start, the more likely she will not object to it as she gets older.

Grooming at Home

Cats should be brushed or combed at least once a week, more often if she goes outside. If you have a long-haired-breed kitten, you can start combing her hair as early as six weeks and should be doing it regularly by ten weeks. If you wait to use a comb until your cat's hair has mats, you will create a negative experience for your kitten as the comb pulls the mats out.

Combing and brushing should be enjoyable for you and kitty. Be gentle and loving, using the comb or brush as an extension of your hand as you stroke the full length of the body. Be sure not to start this at

HOW (OR WHETHER) TO BATHE A CAT

As a rule cats don't need bathing. By nature they keep themselves clean through self-grooming. However, there are times when you may need to bathe your kitten: If he has gotten into a potentially poisonous substance such as paint or pesticide; if you have an allergic person in the house; if you are showing him; if you are dipping him in a flea or tick prevention product; or if for whatever reason he is unusually dirty. Here are some tips:

- Have the sink or tub ready with warm water so the cat isn't traumatized by the look and sound of water running.
- Wear long-sleeved, fairly thick clothing to protect yourself from scratches in case kitty decides to try to escape.
- Put a mat or towel on the bottom of the sink or tub so kitty can grab onto something.
- Put kitty into the water quickly.
- Be sure you are using soap made especially for bathing cats — human soap will dry out their skin and fur.
- Talk softly and reassuringly to the cat as you work in the soap and rinse.
- Towel dry the cat, then let her air dry the rest of the way. Blow dryers frighten most cats.
- Give kitty a treat and lots of praise after her bath.

the beginning of a play period when your kitten is more in "attack" mode. Find a time when she is calmer and affectionate. Consider that even the kitten's mother will not groom them when they are play-fighting. She will wait until they are calm and lying down for a nap.

Be certain to comb all the areas where mats develop. Get under the front legs, between the rear legs, and under the belly. These are all problem areas and you cannot start caring for these areas too early.

Cats go through a shedding period in the spring and fall, and should be brushed or combed more often during those times to keep them free of mats. Making sure that your cat has as little dead hair as possible will also go a long way toward preventing hair balls.

MAT MANAGEMENT

If you see large mats in your cats hair, DO NOT attempt to cut them out unless you have been trained by an experienced groomer. One of the more common cases seen in emergency clinics is the cat that has had its skin laid open by an owner cutting mats out of the hair. The problem is that the cat's skin is very thin and is easily pulled away from the body with the mat. As the owner tries to clip out the mat, they get a bit more than they intended to.

Professional Groomer

While all cats need to be groomed regularly at home, you may choose to take your cat to a professional groomer occasionally. If you plan to do this, now is the best time to start. The initial visit to the groomer may well determine how your cat responds to grooming for the rest of his life; a groomer who is gentle as well as skilled will help your cat adjust to the experience. Of course, a major adjustment may not be necessary, depending on your cat's temperament and whether you have taken the time for regular combing. Remember — the more your cat's hair is matted, the more painful it will be for the groomer to pull the mats out; the additional time and effort may also make the grooming more expensive.

What should you expect (and do) on your kitten's first visit to the groomer? Certainly the cat will get a general clean-up that includes a bath, combing and trimming of too-long hair, removal of "stray" hairs, trimming of the nails, and removal of mats. You should discuss your preferences regarding hair length before turning your cat over to the groomer; this will help avoid confusion, surprise, and possibly anger when you pick up your pet.

If your cat has lots of fleas or ticks, the groomer may apply a dip to help kill any live infestation. As a final word of warning, be aware that if your cat's coat has mats too large to comb out, it may be necessary to shave them out. This is less of a concern on the first visit, since your kitten's hair is probably not yet long enough for heavy mats to form.

TRIMMING YOUR CAT'S NAILS

Keeping your cat's nails trimmed regularly will help keep you and your furniture from being scratched. You can have your vet do this regularly, or you can do it yourself if you feel comfortable.

How to Trim Your Cat's Nails

- Press your cat's paw gently flat to make the claws extend out.
- With your cat sitting or lying down, trim the nails one paw at a time.
- Clip off only the very tips of the nails. The quick (sensitive, blood-filled inner portion) of the nail grows as the nail grows. If you cut too close you will hurt your cat. Work on trimming long nails little by little, over time. If your cat has dark nails it might be difficult to see the quick. Look at the end of the nail straight on (see diagram) and keep your clips tiny until you see a small dark circle. If you clip too far, causing the nail to bleed, apply pressure to the tip.

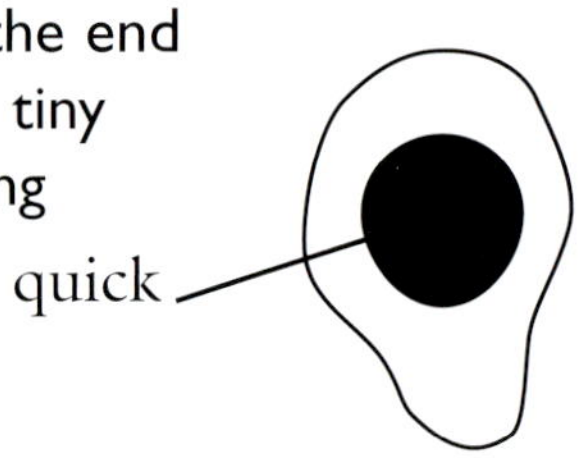

- Give your cat praise and a treat when you're done.

FINAL TOUCH

- Clean your cat's ears with a cotton ball and baby oil or olive oil to remove any accumulated dirt and debris. You should do this about twice a month.

- Clean your cat's eyes with a cotton ball dampened with water. Gently wipe away the discharge or dirt. Do this any time you see that it needs to be done.

FLEA AND TICK PREVENTION

Flea and tick control has long been one of the biggest problems facing pet owners. Anyone who has ever used a collar to prevent or get rid of fleas and ticks knows that they don't work very well. There have been many new products placed on the market recently, many with rather fantastic claims. Lucky for all of us, most of these claims are true. In this section I'll help you get a grasp of which products may be best for you and your pet.

Fleas

Adult female fleas lay eggs that hatch into larvae. These larvae then spin a cocoon and the adult female fleas lay the eggs on the animal. The eggs are very small and white, and fall off the pet wherever he scratches or lies down.

When the eggs hatch, the larvae run from the light and find the darkest place available — the cushions of the couch, under furniture, or other remote corners of your home. These areas are often missed when treating a home for fleas, and once the larvae enter the cocoon, they can resist even the strongest of insecticides and completely infest your home. This entire process takes only 14 to 21 days. In fact, one female in an untreated environment can account

for up to 250,000 offspring! So you can see how you and your pet can quickly become infested with fleas.

The goal of treating a home or a pet is to break the life cycle and keep the numbers manageable. In the past, most insecticides were designed to kill adult fleas. The problems with this plan were (1) that there were ten times as many young adults coming out of the cocoons to replace the adults that were killed and (2) the chemicals were often toxic to the pets. To make matters worse, the adult fleas would develop a resistance to the insecticide. Before long, all that would seem to work was a small nuclear warhead.

At last, some of the pharmaceutical and chemical companies realized there must be a better way to deal with this problem. The focus on treating homes shifted from killing the adults to killing the eggs or the larvae. We now have many choices for effective treatment of fleas in the home. Your exterminator can help you decide which product is best for you. As for killing fleas on your pet, there are many good products available.

FRONTLINE® Top Spot is very effective. In addition to killing fleas, it also kills and repels ticks. It is applied to the skin of the pet. It is dispersed in the oil layer of the skin and stored in the oil glands, where it is slowly released. It continues to be effective for several weeks. The manufacturers of FRONTLINE® also have a solution that kills adult fleas and inactivates the flea eggs. This is FRONTLINE® Plus which is currently the main product this practice recommends for cats.

One female flea in an untreated environment can account for up to 250,000 offspring.

Advantage® claims to kill adult fleas within 24 to 48 hours of contact with a treated animal. The idea with this product is that the adult flea will not live long enough to lay eggs. We have seen better results with other products if the pet must be bathed regularly, but Advantage® seems to be a promising product in certain circumstances.

PROGRAM™ uses a revolutionary method of treating the adult fleas and sterilizing the adult females. The medication is given once a month with a meal. The compound is absorbed like fat and stored in the fat layers of the pet's body. Since even thin animals have some fat under the skin, the flea will contact the drug each time it takes a blood meal and destroy all the eggs. No eggs. Then, no fleas.

The focus on treating homes has shifted from killing the adults to killing the eggs or the larvae.

This product has worked well for many of our clients. A disadvantage is that if you have a flea-allergic animal, an allergic reaction will be started each time a flea bites. The plan should be to keep the pet on PROGRAM™ all year long to prevent the flea population from reaching significant numbers.

CAPSTAR™ is another adulticide product. This product is given orally and begins to take effect within 30 minutes. This product is best used with PROGRAM™ to provide a complete control system.

Even with the development of these wonderful products, treatment of the outdoors with insecticides still has a place in total flea control in any particular environment. In cases of heavy infestation, consulting a professional exterminator may be in order.

Ticks

Ticks are a serious threat to the health of pets and pet owners. They are hard-bodied, blood-sucking parasites that generally live outdoors but have been known to infest buildings. They are known to carry Lyme Disease, Rocky Mountain Spotted Fever, Ehrlichiosis, Babesia, Bartonella, and other significant health threats. Ticks are usually found on pets and people who participate in outdoor activities or pets that live outdoors in infested yards. Control can be difficult since ticks can survive for long periods without a blood meal.

If your home or yard is infested, contacting a professional exterminator will give you the greatest chance of clearing up the problem. Preventing infestation of your home by preventing your animal from bringing in the pest is an important step in control.

For tick control on your kitten, FRONTLINE® Top Spot is the most effective I have seen. Applied to the back of your cat periodically, it kills the tick once it contacts the pet. It is effective against several types of ticks and appears to be the

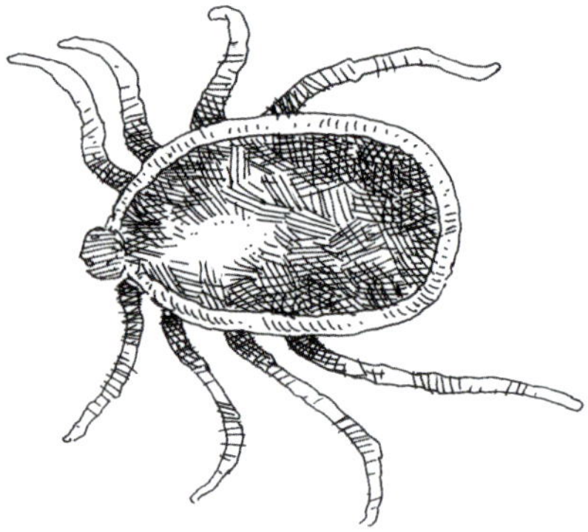

best prevention for general infestation.

Revolution® provides effective protection against one type of tick and has limited usefulness in preventing infestation in heavy exposure situations with multiple species. The benefit of Revolution® is that it also prevents fleas and heartworms and is fully absorbed

into the system within two hours.

Many pet owners mistakenly believe that Advantage® and PROGRAM™ prevent ticks. Neither of these products has any effect on ticks.

If your home or yard is infested, contacting a professional exterminator will give you the greatest chance of clearing the problem.

FLEA AND TICK PRODUCTS AT A GLANCE

Treat your cat for fleas and ticks, especially if she goes outdoors.If you find that she has fleas or ticks, have your home treated so that any that escape will not be able to take over your home.

Topical treatments

- FRONTLINE® Top Spot (flea and tick repellent applied monthly)
- Advantage® (flea control applied monthly)
- Revolution® (monthly control of fleas, ticks, and prevents heartworms)

Ingested treatments

- PROGRAM™ (flea "adulticide" given once monthly with a meal)
- CAPSTAR™ (flea "adulticide" sometimes given in conjunction with PROGRAM™)

WEEK 8 CHECKLIST

- ✓ Begin to groom your cat while she is young.
- ✓ Brush or comb your kitty at least once a week.
- ✓ Give your kitten a bath to get her comfortable around water.
- ✓ Learn how to trim your cat's nails.
- ✓ Choose a pest prevention product and use it regularly.

Kitten Development: Week 8

- Kittens should be fully weaned.
- Kittens should begin learning to drink from a dish.
- Kitty will still be socially attached to the mother and other kittens if not yet adopted.

Notes:

Notes:

Week 9: Toys & Playing

Just like a human child, your kitten is going to want plenty of things to play with. Cats particularly enjoy hunting, chasing, pouncing, sneaking up on things, and exploring new spaces. Your goal should be to provide kitty with places and objects that satisfy her playful curiosity without getting her into trouble.

One of the neatest things about kittens is that they are fascinated by the simplest of items. It's sort of like the young child that gets a big, new toy — in a box. What does the child play with? Is it the nice new toy that took three hours to assemble or … the box? You guessed it! The box will win out most of the time. I've been amazed at the kittens that get a new toy but would rather play with the foam packing peanuts instead.

KITTEN TOY TIPS

Small balls are a particular favorite of many kittens — even balled-up bits of paper. They also like small, foam-rubber balls because they can carry them in their mouth. This type of toy is not only something your kitten will enjoy playing with — they come in handy

One of the neatest things about kittens is that they are fascinated by the simplest of items.

TOY SELECTION

YES:

- Balls
- Paper balls
- Plastic milk jugs
- Scratching posts
- Cat furniture
- Bell toys (if the bell is large enough not to be swallowed)
- Feathered toys
- Paper bags
- Toy mice
- Catnip toys

NO:

- Rubber bands
- Plastic bags
- String of any kind, including yarn
- Plastic rings from milk jugs
- Coins
- Beads
- Buttons
- Tinsel
- Mylar
- Anything with small parts
- Anything small enough to swallow

as distractions that lure your kitten away from otherwise annoying play behavior.

For example, often a kitten will dart out from under furniture and attack his owners' feet. One solution I found for that is to keep several small balls in a basket on either end of the room the kitten uses to stalk the feet. If I know that the kitten is in attack mode, I'll pick up a ball, roll it in front of my feet and let the ball be the recipient of the attack

Curiosity will almost always get the best of a kitten that sees a paper bag lying open.

instead of my legs. I have found that ping pong balls work well because they are light enough that a single swat will send them sailing across the room and totally preoccupy the kitten.

If your kitten likes balls then you may consider getting one of the toys that has a ball inside a track where the kitten can reach into the track to swat the ball but the ball does not get tossed all over the house.

Another good toy is a simple paper bag. (CAUTION — AVOID PLASTIC BAGS AS TOYS. Small animals and children can suffocate in plastic bags.) Curiosity will almost

always get the best of a kitten that sees a paper bag lying open. If you create a small rustling sound by scratching the outside bottom of the bag, the kitten will often simply attack the bag. What a blast! Fun for the whole family.

Perhaps the best use of laser technology is hand-held laser pointers that become cat toys. Kittens and adult cats will chase laser spots for hours. You can make the light appear to go under furniture and pop out on the other side. You can simulate the activities of a mouse or a small bug. Once you get your cat convinced the "mouse" is under the table, she will often wait for a long time for the prey to show itself again.

A word of caution: avoid shining the pointer into the eyes of either animals or humans to avoid damaging the eyes.

TOYS TO AVOID

Forget the image of a cute little kitten playing with a ball of yarn. You should avoid any sort of string as a toy. Strings can be deadly because they can actually get wrapped around the base of the tongue or become lodged in the stomach with a trailing end traveling into the intestines. As the intestines attempt to pull the string through it becomes taut and can actually cut through tissue much like a wire

THE VET'S NOTEBOOK

Play Time Is Serious!

Cats are social, playful animals by nature, and your willingness to play with your cat can make the difference between a happy, loving cat, and a bored, under-socialized behavior problem. As important as toys are, they aren't much fun for your cat to play with alone. You should play with your indoor cats at least two hours a day, and socialize your animal either with another cat, or by spending time with her yourself.

Through play, cats learn proper social skills, coordination, and timing, and they gain the intellectual stimulation that they crave. A bored cat may eventually become aggressive out of a desire for attention or simply out of frustration.

While play time with your cat is always special, you MUST choose appropriate toys. Balls, paper bags, and boxes are great choices for play, but plastic bags, rubber bands, or any kind of string is dangerous for your cat. String can cause serious intestinal distress in a cat and is difficult to diagnose. Almost any time a cat is vomiting, your veterinarian should start looking for some sort of intestinal obstruction.

One of the most troubled patients I have ever had was a cat who had chewed a shoelace off of an ice skate and swallowed it. The shoelace, like most string, didn't show up in an X-ray, and didn't show up after contrast material was put into the cat's intestines. The next step was to cut the cat open in order to find the obstruction. The shoelace swallower survived, but many string-eaters don't. You can save yourself a lot of heartbreak — and save your cat's life — by choosing playthings other than string. Rubber bands and hair ties are just as bad. Or, if you do choose toys that have strings or loose parts attached to them, be sure kitty is supervised while she plays, then put the toys away when playtime is over.

cheese cutter cuts through cheese.

This, of course, can be lethal once the string opens the wall of the intestine into the abdomen. Many cat toys have objects attached to a pole with string. I don't have a problem with these for supervised play. Just be sure they are stored where they are inaccessible to the kitten when you aren't around.

One more warning: If your kitten seems to go wild during playtime, be certain none of your toys have catnip in them. I have seen perfectly loving cats become crazed hellions when exposed to catnip. Most cats enjoy catnip from time to time; there are also a small percentage who are immune to the plant. But if your kitten is behaving strangely, she could be one of those who over-react. If this is the case you should withhold catnip.

WEEK 9 CHECKLIST

✓ Play with your kitten every day.

✓ Buy or make your kitten some toys, but make sure they're safe.

✓ If your cat is over-stimulated, check his toys for catnip.

✓ Your cat should have his first round of vaccinations around 9-10 weeks.

Kitten Development: Week 9

- Kitten may begin to play more aggressively in preparation for adult hunting and fighting.
- It's time for several vaccines this week.

Week 10: Claws 101

By now, your kitten is probably exploring your home freely, and will use her claws to help her stabilize herself when she jumps on your sofa, on your lap, or even while she's climbing your curtains. Kittens will also use their claws to "catch" balls or other toys while playing. It doesn't take long to realize that these sharp instruments can damage many of your belongings in no time.

CLAW MANAGEMENT

Trimming

There are several ways you can deal with the problem. The first is to keep the claws trimmed regularly. As long as you start early and get your kitty used to this every week or so, she probably won't mind too much. Have your vet show you how to do this safely and easily.

The other way to deal with your kitty's claws is to get her a scratching post. Cats naturally work on sharpening their claws continually. So as soon as you or your vet cuts them back, she will immediately go to work getting them sharp again. You'll have to teach her that a scratching post is the appropriate place for her to sharpen her claws, and that the back of your couch is not.

Scratching Post

A good scratching post should be covered with a material that is attractive to the kitten — sisal rope, carpet, a bare surface, or a

SCRATCHING POST TIPS

- Don't cover the scratching post with the fabric that you're training the cat to avoid.
- An easy homemade scratching post can be created by mounting a small wooden log on a flat base piece and securing it tightly enough that it won't fall onto your cat and hurt him.
- Cats don't like surfaces that catch their claws, like open weave fabrics or netting. Cover your cat's favorite scratching spots with these, not their scratching post.
- Praise and positive reinforcement for correct behavior is more effective than punishment for incorrect behavior.

combination of all three. You can also make one out of a wooden log.

Don't cover the scratching post with the fabric that you're trying to train the cat to avoid — this will just confuse her. Much like litter box training, scratching post training requires some supervision.

First, cover some of your cat's favorite inappropriate scratching areas, such as a couch or shelf, with netting or open weave fabric that will snag her claws. Cats don't like the feeling of a snagged claw and this will dissuade her from scratching this piece of furniture in the future.

Confine your cat in a single room or two rooms with at least one scratching post. The more options she has the more she will learn to enjoy the posts rather than the drapes. Praise and reward her whenever she scratches the

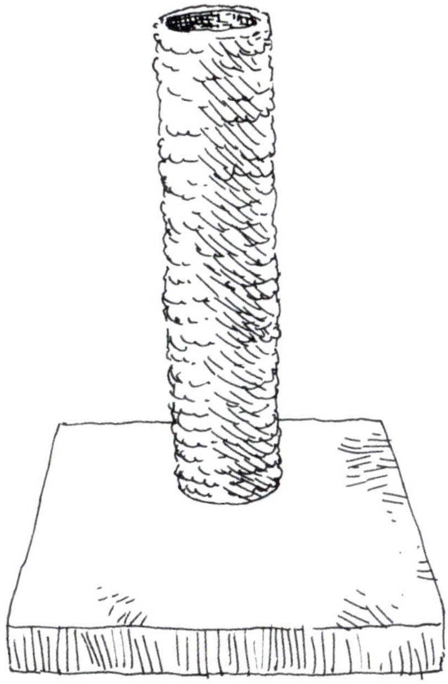

appropriate items. If she isn't interested at first, try dangling toys from the posts, putting treats on top of them, or rubbing them with catnip. Encourage your cat every time she correctly uses the posts. Negative reinforcement is not recommended.

The last thing to remember about a scratching post is that some cats just don't use them no matter what you do, and trying to make a cat do something she isn't inclined to do is probably, well, like trying to herd cats.

CLAWS — SHOULD KITTY KEEP THEM?

Declawing a cat has always been a controversial issue. Most professional veterinary organizations strongly discourage the removal of any body part for cosmetic reasons or any other reason other than the health of the animal. In fact, there is a large push to have declawing outlawed. Personally, I strongly discourage any cat owner from removing the claws, for several reasons.

The first reason is the trauma involved. The surgery is more invasive than many people think,

TO DECLAW, OR NOT TO DECLAW?

Declawing should NEVER be considered for an outdoor cat, or even for an indoor cat who occasionally goes outside. This puts him in danger by taking away his main line of defense and preventing him from escaping situations (by climbing).

Many cat lovers and veterinarians consider declawing cruel, since it is usually painful for the cat, and in most cases is unnecessary. If the problem you are experiencing is the clawing of furniture, try training your cat with a spray bottle, or talk to your vet about alternative solutions.

Another factor to consider when having a cat declawed is whether or not you'll ever have to give the cat away. If you become sick, have to move to a place where no pets are allowed, or have to give the cat away for other reasons, you need to consider whether or not future owners will ensure that she never gets outside.

since it is actually an amputation at the last knuckle. The second reason is that cats use their claws for play and other tasks, almost like we use our fingers.

The surgery is more invasive than many people think, since it is actually an amputation at the last knuckle.

Another important reason I don't recommend declawing is that if a cat finds herself outside (either intentionally on your part or because she escaped), she will have a tough time protecting or defending herself.

Many veterinarians still perform this procedure, due to the realization that if they don't, another veterinarian will. (Of course, some vets are more concerned about the size of the invoice than the well-being of the patient.)

This stance would not be defensible if the practice were outlawed. Until that time arrives, if you feel that you must pursue this action, please take the time to educate yourself about the different types of procedures, and find someone who uses the least traumatic procedure. Most vets only remove the front claws, as these are the ones cats use to ruin furniture. They then still have their back claws for climbing.

The bottom line is that this is a decision you'll have to make for yourself, depending on whether or not your cat will go outside, how much you love your furniture, and whether or not you think declawing is inhumane.

WEEK 10 CHECKLIST

✓ Keep your kitten's claws trimmed regularly.

✓ Buy your kitten a scratching post, and teach her to use it.

✓ If you plan to have your kitty declawed, research all of your options before making this drastic (and final) decision – most problems with claws can be solved without removing the claws.

Kitten Development: Week 2

- Kittens should be completely vaccinated before being let outside.
- Kitty's weight continues to increase, and a growth spurt may soon occur.

Week 11: Basic Health Care

EXAMINE YOUR CAT REGULARLY

It goes without saying that there is no substitute for qualified veterinary care for your kitten. However, you can go a long way toward supporting your vet's efforts — and preventing illness and even emergencies — by learning to spot the typical signs of health or illness in your cat.

Start by familiarizing yourself with every part of your cat's body. Getting your kitten used to your touch at an early age is always a good idea. It will make her more cooperative later on when it comes time to groom, administer medication, or handle her for any other reason.

Gently touch and examine your cat's head and ears, neck, body, legs, feet, and tail. Open her m ·th and rub her teeth and gums a finger. (A neat trick tc her used to you opening her uth is to insert a treat w u do this.) Familiarize f with what a healthy and feels like.

If ce problems in any are r veterinarian a call. It may be nothing, but it's always better to be safe than sorry.

KNOW WHAT NOT TO DO

Some owners make the mistake of confusing caring with overindulging. Don't let that happen to you. Yes, this is your little baby, your precious pride and joy —

You want to always avoid giving your kitten table scraps.

and that is exactly why you should refrain from certain indulgences that may seem loving but in reality can harm or even kill your pet.

In general, you want to always avoid giving your kitten table scraps. As hard as it is to resist her big pleading eyes for a bite of shrimp or chicken, table scraps are a richer diet than is good for your cat. Too many rich human treats can lead to liver, kidney, and pancreas problems. Those are the kinds of problems that can cost you literally thousands of dollars in veterinary bills and can even cost you the life of your pet.

Do not ever give a pet human edication (ibuprofen, aspirin, etaminophen). Don't leave her thout water, or leave her in a parked car with the windows shut.

In general, just use common sense. Our pets very quickly get all tangled up in our emotions and sometimes it isn't all that easy to see what is, or is not, in your kitty's best interest. Your kitten sure can't see it, so it's up to you.

LEARN TO SPOT A PROBLEM

There are some classic signs and symptoms of illness that you should familiarize yourself with. I can't tell you how many times distressed owners of sick cats have come into my clinic saying, "If only I'd known..."

Cats can't tell us when they don't feel so good, so it often seems that serious illnesses just blossom

BASIC HEALTH CARE AT A GLANCE

Remember, you know your cat best.

- Observe her regularly for changes in behavior, eating habits, or elimination habits.
- Examine her body regularly for problems with the skin or coat, lumps or abnormal growths, and tenderness to your touch.
- Examine inside your cat's mouth for signs of gum disease or other dental problems.
- If you observe coughing or sneezing, discharge of any kind, fluctuation in weight, head shaking, or drooling, call your vet.
- Don't feed your cat table scraps.
- Be aware of how the weather and other conditions may affect your cat.
- DO NOT give your cat any human medications without detailed instructions from your vet.

overnight into full-blown crises. "But he was fine yester[illegible] is another one I hear a[illegible] in reality, the cat was not fi[illegible] it was just that the owner didn't [illegible] anything until the cat was so [illegible]hat his behavior became ext[illegible]ut of character. You can hel[illegible]his situation by understandi[illegible] taking seriously, some of the classic early symptoms of illness.

The most important thing to watch for is any change in behavior that is out of character.

The most important thing to watch for is any change in behavior that is out of character. Lethargy and withdrawal in particular can often mean your cat doesn't feel well. Eating and drinking habits that are not your cat's usual can signal any number of problems; the longer such symptoms persist the more chance there is that something is wrong. Unusual discharge from any part of the body, coughing, excessive licking or panting, excessive drooling, urinating too

much or not enough, extensive vomiting or diarrhea, abnormally bad breath, yelping or whimpering when touched, repeated head shaking or scratching — all of these should catch your attention and cause you to be concerned. That doesn't mean you should panic; you should, however, continue to pay attention and if the symptoms persist, see your vet.

TAKE THE SEASONS INTO ACCOUNT

You wouldn't go out without a warm coat in winter, and you wouldn't go out with a warm coat in summer. The same applies to your cat. Young kittens especially are susceptible to heat and cold, and to conditions that can be triggered by excessive heat or cold or overexposure to the elements. Use sense when the weather is cold or hot. This section will give you some tips.

Warm weather

Cat owners often overlook the threat of heat stroke. Remember — one reason human beings can adjust to hot weather with relatively little difficulty is that we have sweat glands throughout our bodies to help keep our internal thermostats regulated; cats do not.

In fact, the only places a cat sweats are the nose and foot pads. Cats mostly lose heat by moving warmed air out of their lungs and breathing in cooler air — this is why cats pant when they are hot. Because this is an inefficient way of regulating body temperature, most cats are prone to heat exhaustion. A

cat can become overheated by being outside on a hot summer day. You can protect your kitten from heat stroke by keeping a close watch on his activities during hot weather, and making sure he gets plenty of water.

Being left in a car in warm weather can also cause heat stroke in cats. When a car's air conditioner is turned off on a hot day, the temperature in the car rises very quickly, and a partially lowered window is not adequate to offset the rising heat. The amount of heat is exacerbated if your pet is in a carrier.

When taking your cat to and from the vet, try not to make any stops on the way.

When taking your cat to and from the vet, try not to make any stops on the way where you will have to leave your cat in the car. If you want to get some idea of how being left in a hot car can affect your cat, just try it yourself one day. My guess is that after about 10 minutes in the sweltering summer heat you'll know why the practice can be deadly.

Cold weather

Winter and the holiday season present several potential problems for our pets. Here are several points to remember.

If your cat lives outside, be certain that he has good protection from the wind and rain. When the temperature drops into the twenties, most animals will need to have some additional shelter or a place to stay in the garage or basement. This will reduce the stress an animal experiences and will help keep them healthy.

There are many poisons that make winter and the holidays a dangerous time. Remember to dispose of your antifreeze properly when you change it in your car. Even a small amount makes a deadly drink for your pet. Many decorative plants, such as poinsettias, are also a serious threat.

Frozen water is another common problem in the winter. If you keep your pet's water outside, be certain it stays warm enough to be liquid. Outdoor pets often get dehydrated in the winter because their only source of water is frozen. Drinking Christmas tree water is another danger of the holidays, especially if you put chemicals in it to prolong the life of the tree. I recommend not adding chemicals, since it can be very hard to keep a cat out of the water.

BASIC FIRST AID

Your knowledge of some basic first aid measures can make the difference between life and death for your kitten in a critical situation. First, realize that any injured animal is inclined to bite, with no regard for how well they know the person attempting to help them.

If you are attempting to administer aid to your cat, use a heavy blanket or an article of clothing to shield the arm nearest the cat's head.

If you are attempting to administer aid to your cat, use a heavy blanket or an article of clothing to shield the arm nearest the cat's head. This protection will allow you to make contact with her to check out her injuries, as well as providing some comfort.

Once the injured cat is secured against injuring the caregiver, the next step in applying first aid is assessing the most critical aspects of the injury. Is the cat breathing? If so, how effectively? Is the breathing

BASIC FIRST AID AT A GLANCE

Be prepared ahead of time:

- Know your vet's emergency number or the location of your local emergency veterinary clinic.
- Post the animal poison control number on your refrigerator o bulletin board (888) 4ANIHELP.
- Have your vet show you how to administer feline CPR.

If your cat is injured:

- Protect yourself from a potential bite or scratch from the injured cat while you are examining him.
- Try to stop any major bleeding.
- Check his airways if he isn't bleeding.

shallow, very rapid, or coming with a congested sound? If so, the animal should be transported as quickly as possible (within the bounds of safety, of course) to the nearest emergency veterinary facility.

Inadequate air exchange is often the result of damage to the lungs or trachea, and can claim a cat's life in less than the time it may take you to reach a vet. On the other hand, if you notice that the cat's attempts to breathe are resulting in no air moving through his nose or mouth, check the cat's mouth for an object lodged there. This may help avoid a trip to the emergency room — but bear in mind the possibility of being bitten when you put your hand in the cat's mouth, particularly if you're dealing with an animal that is struggling against you.

You should also look for any lacerations or other signs of bleeding. If bleeding is present, is it flowing freely or gushing from the wound? If so, it must be stopped immediately to reduce the likelihood of the cat dying from blood loss. Generally, direct pressure on a bleeding wound is the first step in controlling loss of blood.

Learn how to administer feline cardiopulmonary resuscitation (CPR).

You should be aware that if there is a broken bone, the bleeding may be due to a bone fragment having severed an artery. In this case, direct pressure on the area of the fracture can cause further damage to the blood vessel, or to nerves in the area. In these situations, the best approach is to apply pressure to an appendage in an area between the wound and the heart.

I recommend

HOW TO GIVE A CAT MEDICINE

PILLS

- Don't crush or mix in food unless your vet says it's okay.
- Place the kitten or cat on your lap or a high surface such as a counter.
- Grasp the head just below the cheekbones and tip the head up.
- Hold the pill between thumb and forefinger of your other hand and with a third finger, gently pry open kitty's mouth.
- Drop or place the pill quickly as far down the throat as possible, keeping the head tipped back.
- Rub and stroke the throat, telling kitty what a good cat she is.
- Give your kitten a treat and lots more praise.
- Don't try this while your kitten is eating.

LIQUIDS

- Mixing them in food may not work since your kitten will smell them.
- Make sure the dropper is nearby, already full of the correct amount of medicine.
- Hold the cat on your lap or a counter facing away from you.
- Grasp the head and pry open the mouth as you would when giving a pill, and squeeze the medicine in.
- Stroke the throat with the head back, as when giving pills.
- Give a treat and lots of praise.

ANOTHER METHOD

Another method of giving medicine that works well with some kittens and cats is to wrap the animal in a towel. Pick kitty up with his back against your chest, holding the front legs of the animal down and close to his own chest with one arm. Take a bath towel with your other hand and wrap it tightly around kitty, slipping out the arm that was holding kitty's front legs down. Pry the mouth open, and quickly administer the medication.

Afterwards, hold the swaddled kitty close to you and pet and stroke and praise him. Give a treat and release.

It is very important to give your cat food and water after giving him medication. This will force the medication out of the esophagus and in to the stomach.

WHAT TO DO IF YOUR CAT IS POISONED

Call your local vet, or The National Animal Poison Control Center at (888) 4ANIHELP (426-4435) (Visa, MasterCard, Discover, or American Express required) or (900) 443-0000. Note: there is a $50 fee for this service. The Center will do as many follow-up calls as necessary in critical cases, and at the owner's request will contact their veterinarian. The Center also provides via fax specific treatment protocols and current literature citations when indicated.

that you also take the time to learn how to administer feline cardiopulmonary resuscitation (CPR). There are numerous outstanding books on feline first aid, as well as a plethora of information available through various reputable veterinary, humane, and breed-related websites. Remember — the time to familiarize yourself with the techniques of feline first aid is NOT as an emergency occurs. Consider asking your vet to host a pet first aid class at his office, where he can demonstrate some basic measures that could save your cat's life.

Unfortunately, owners often attempt to medicate their kitten using human medication. While many of the medications used in veterinary medicine are the same as those used in human medicine, the doses are often extremely different. NEVER attempt to medicate your kitten unless you have specific instructions from your veterinarian.

WHEN TO SEE YOUR VET

Cats, much like humans, deal with sickness and injury in different ways. Some cats will display obvious signs that something is wrong, while others will try to hide their discomfort. The key to recognizing an injury or illness is knowing your cat's normal behavior well enough to recognize a change.

Keep a close eye on her appetite, the amount of water she drinks, and how often she urinates or defecates. Any changes in the norm can signal a problem. By the time you notice that your cat looks thin, she may have already lost a significant amount of body mass. Becoming lethargic, straining,

THE VET'S NOTEBOOK

A Note About Toxoplasmosis

Toxoplasmosis is a one-cell parasitic organism that uses cats as its primary host. These organisms are passed in the feline feces and become infectious within three days. They can cause serious problems if a pregnant woman is infected in the earlier stages of her pregnancy, including severe irreversible damage to the retina of the fetus. Many cats have lost families because obstetricians have counseled cat owners to rid themselves of their pets.

This is simply not necessary. Many of us are already exposed and have protective antibodies against this organism. If your antibody level is high, then you are probably safe from this organism. The only way your cat will have this organism is if he lives outside and kills and eats prey. Even then, your cat is not going to infect you by simply being in contact with you. This parasite has a fecal-oral life cycle. This means that as long as you wash your hands well between cleaning out the litter box and eating food with your hands, your threat is almost totally removed. Finally, if your cat has this organism it won't become infectious for a few days, so if you clean the box daily, it removes the risk.

I am not suggesting that you not follow you obstetrician's advice, just that you ask plenty of questions and research the topic before taking any rash actions.

Just to be on the safe side, ask a spouse, friend, or neighbor to help out with litter box duties while you're pregnant. If you don't have help to keep the litter box clean, wear rubber gloves when changing the litter and thoroughly wash your hands afterwards. And change your cat's litter on a daily basis.

panting, limping, sensitivity to touch, disorientation, runny or watery eyes, bloody discharge, coughing, sneezing, hard or sensitive belly, excessive accidents in the house, vomiting, cuts, loss of fur, or skin difficulties are just a few symptoms that you can look for.

In the end you just have to go with your gut. If a behavior or change in your cat makes you anxious, it can't hurt to give your vet a call. Remember, early detection is the key to healing most feline illnesses.

WEEK 11 CHECKLIST

- ✓ Do a total-body exam on your cat, and get familiar with how your healthy cat feels and looks.
- ✓ Know what not to do to keep your kitten healthy.
- ✓ Know the signs of illness.
- ✓ Learn some of the common hazards to your kitty in cold and hot weather.
- ✓ Learn basic first aid, including CPR, for your cat.

Week 12: Dental Care

Many people believe that feeding your cat dry food or a tartar control food will eliminate the need to brush his or her teeth. This goes against common sense! If I were to tell you that if you ate a dry, shredded wheat biscuit daily you would never need to brush your teeth again, you would think I was nuts! Why would you believe that about your cat? While eating a strict diet of dry food reduces the amount of cleaning your cat's teeth needs, it does not eliminate the need for dental care.

DENTAL DISEASE

Dental disease is very common in cats. The most common ailments you must be aware of are periodontal disease and pyorrhea. The buildup of plaque and tartar on the teeth causes bacteria to grow in the gum tissue. This bacteria, in turn, produces chemicals that irritate the gum and leads to damage of the supporting structure for the tooth. Eventually infection spreads into the gum tissue itself and then the tooth will loosen. In some cases the infection leads to abscess formation and serious pain for the cat. Eventually, a cat will lose an infected tooth.

HOME CARE OF YOUR CAT'S TEETH

I suggest that you brush your cat's teeth about three times a week if at all possible. Take it slowly as you train your cat to accept you working in his mouth. Simply rubbing the front teeth in a small area and then giving him his favorite treat is a good way to start. Slowly expand the area you are rubbing until you can cover all the teeth.

Simply rubbing the front teeth in a small area and then giving him his favorite treat is a good way to start.

TIPS FOR BRUSHING YOUR CAT'S TEETH

- Place your cat on a counter or table, with his head away from you.
- Using a cat toothbrush or finger cot with cat toothpaste on it, slowly lift up your cat's upper lip and rub the outside surface of the back teeth. Don't worry if your cat won't open his mouth, just get the outside surface.
- If your cat becomes upset, just leave him alone and try again when he calms down, or even the next day.
- No matter how much or little you accomplish, reward your kitty with a treat when you're done.

(Most cats will not let you open their mouths to brush the inside surface of the teeth, so you want to keep the mouth closed and concentrate on the outside surface of the teeth.)

Then, add a dollop of the special pet toothpaste and start again. Cats

STAGES OF GUM DISEASE

Gingivitis: Inflammation of the gums caused by plaque. Gums are slightly red and swollen. Breath may be slightly unpleasant.

Early Periodontitis: Plaque and tartar are more noticeable. Tartar may extend under the gums. Breath is noticeably unpleasant. Gum edges are red and swollen.

Moderate Periodontitis: Plaque and tartar cover most of the teeth and extend under the gum edges. Breath is extremely unpleasant. Gums may bleed easily. Bacteria from the gums can enter the bloodstream and damage organs.

Advanced Periodontitis: Thick tartar covers teeth. Breath is terribly offensive. Supporting bone has been damaged. Teeth loosen and eventually fall out.

keep the inside surfaces of their teeth fairly clean with their tongue, so the outside surface is the only part you really need to worry about.

If you do this on a daily basis as you are training your kitten, he should soon be willing to have his teeth brushed every two to three days.

PROFESSIONAL CLEANINGS

If your cat simply will not let you clean his teeth regularly at home, you should consider having them professionally cleaned about once a year. Have your vet take a look at your cat's teeth, and he can tell you if this is necessary. Some cats take well to professional cleanings, but most have to be sedated for it to be done properly. Talk with your vet about the best method of sedation for your cat.

BAD BREATH

There are many things that can cause your cat to have smelly breath.

Teething

At about 6 months of age, cats lose their baby teeth and get permanent ones. The gums may get

Some cats take well to professional cleanings, but most have to be sedated for it to be done properly.

red and puffy, and you should be able to see the points of teeth breaking through in places. You may also find the baby teeth lying around your house. Teething can cause an odor, but it will go away when the new teeth come in.

Gum disease

If the gums appear red and puffy and you've ruled out teething, your cat may have a gum infection. You should have you vet take a look at this immediately.

Diet

Certain foods, usually canned foods or prescription foods, can make your cat's breath smell. If possible, try changing your cat's diet.

Abscessed tooth

If your cat has an abscessed tooth, you may not be able to tell by looking in his mouth. If your cat has extremely bad breath and you don't think it's teething or his food, you should have your vet take a look. Sometimes cats drool when they have an abscessed tooth, but not always. If he has an abscess, it will have to be drained, and it's possible that the tooth will have to be removed. If infection from an abscess spreads, it can cause swelling in your cat's face.

WEEK 12 CHECKLIST

✓ Learn to brush your cat's teeth – the earlier you start the easier this will be.

✓ Know the symptoms of dental disease in your kitty.

✓ Talk to your vet about professional cleanings – he'll tell you when/if they are necessary for your cat.

✓ Your cat should have his second round of vaccinations around 12-14 weeks.

Notes:

Notes:

Week 13: Read the Signs

While cats are domesticated animals, they have not been as thoroughly domesticated as dogs. Most cats still have a very strong instinct for self-preservation. That means, if it comes down to you or them, you'll probably lose out.

For this reason, it would be a good idea for you to make an effort to learn your cat's mood signals. The most loving cat in the world would scratch you if you, say, broke up a fight. Cats that are already in over-stimulated, nervous, or frightening situations will likely react negatively if you try to touch them or pick them up. The "fight or flight" instinct is very strong in these situations, and your cat will act accordingly.

If a cat is seated and flicks her tail back and forth, this usually indicates irritation.

You should be able to recognize irritation on the part of your cat. If he wants to be left alone, then giving him some space is usually advisable. Do remember, however, that sudden changes in personality may point to a medical problem, so know your cat's normal behavior well.

CAT LANGUAGE

Visual Signals

Tails

When your cat's tail is straight up in the air, this is a signal that she is happy and receptive to petting or attention from you or other animals. This can also be a request for food.

If a cat is seated and flicks her tail back and forth, this usually indicates irritation. If you're petting your cat and she starts to do this, it is probably a signal that petting-time is over. If you ignore this signal from a cat, she may eventually bite or hiss at you to give you a stronger message.

Tail switching can also be the prelude to a fight between two cats, right before they pounce. A tail that is held down with an elevated rump indicates aggression, usually toward another cat. A fluffed-up, arched tail with an arched back is a familiar image to most of us. This means that a cat is scared, and torn between being aggressive or defensive. A fluffed tail that is positioned straight out or down indicates that the cat has chosen aggression.

If you're petting your cat and she starts to switch her tail back and forth, it is probably a signal that petting time is over.

A cat's tail wrapped around his body usually indicates that he is content and probably about to settle down for a nap.

Ears

Cats are very expressive animals, and one way they express their feeling is with ear position. When approaching an enemy, if a cat's ears are lying flat against his head, this usually indicates defensiveness.

Ears that are lying flat with just the points visible from the front indicate that he is the aggressor. Forward-pointing ears indicate confidence and curiosity, usually by a cat listening for sounds in front of him. If a cat is hunting prey (like, say, a toy mouse), his ears will be pointing forward to collect all the noises around him. This gives him an advantage, since cats have excellent hearing.

Eyes

A cat's eyes aren't as easy to read as his tail, but there isn't much to know. The first thing to be aware of is that cats do not like to hold eye contact. A continuous stare makes cats defensive and uncomfortable, and they will usually look away if

THE VET'S NOTEBOOK

Careful with that Catnip!

I've heard a lot of people say that catnip doesn't really do anything to cats, but there's no doubt that something's going on there! While I don't know the chemical properties of catnip, my experience as a cat owner and veterinarian has taught me that a lot of kitties have a very strong reaction to the plant.

I once had a feline patient whose owners brought her to my office to board several times a year. She was always a very sweet cat after she had been in the office for two or three days, but when the kitty arrived — whew! She always seemed to be in attack mode during the first several hours of her stay.

The change in the kitty's personality was so dramatic that I suspected catnip was the culprit. "Do you give catnip to your cat before bringing her to the office?" I asked. "No," her owner replied. "Does she have any toys with catnip in them?" Again, the answer was no. Yet when the cat came for routine office visits, she always exhibited the same troublesome behavior. Even the stress of traveling in the carrier or visiting the vet shouldn't turn an ordinary kitty into a crazy wildcat, so I decided to investigate further. The owners always brought their cat to my office in the same carrier. When cat and owner next visited my office, I peeked inside the carrier and spotted a tiny cloth mouse. "Did you know this mouse was in the carrier?" I asked the owner. "We had forgotten all about that toy!" she exclaimed. Sure enough, the little mouse had catnip stuffing. We removed the toy from the carrier and on all the following visits, kitty acted sweet for the duration of her stay.

If your cat has unpredictable behavior problems, check all the toys for catnip content. You may be surprised at the difference in your pet's behavior. Of course, not all cats have a bad reaction to catnip. Some enjoy it without turning troublesome, and there's no toxicity factor at all. But with other cats, you may just have to be prepared for some out-of-control behavior!

you try to engage them in a stareoff. This is why a cat will sometimes ignore all the cat lovers in a room who want his attention, and instead go toward the person who doesn't like cats — he is going toward the one who isn't looking at him.

The slow eye blink or half-closed eye is your cat's way of saying he is content and trusting. He will do this to humans and other cats to indicate that all is well. A slow eye blink from you indicates the same to your cat, and will make him feel even more secure.

If a cat is in a fight or feeling defensive, his pupils will be dilated to provide him with wider peripheral vision, an advantage in anticipating an attack. The aggressor's pupils narrow to give him better depth perception, an advantage in judging where to attack.

The slow eye blink is your cat's way of saying he is content and trusting.

Like the human eye, your cat's eyes will also dilate to let in more light if they are in a dark place.

Vocal Signals

Purring

There is nothing quite like curling up with a purring cat on your lap. For most of us, this is the sound of contentment. While purring usually does indicate that your cat is content and relaxed, it may also indicate other cat emotions or physical conditions. Some cats purr when they are nervous or frightened, and some cats purr when they are sick. So, while you should be happy to hear the sound of your cat purring, if her other behavior indicates that something isn't right you should pay close attention to what is going on.

Meowing

Cats usually meow when they want attention. It's their way of saying, "Hey, I need something." Cats will usually seek you out and meow if they want to play, need food or water, or are trying to tell you something else (like, hey, my toy is stuck under the couch).

If a cat gets locked in a closet or other room by mistake, is outside and wants in, or is in trouble somehow, he will usually meow louder, and continuously, until someone pays attention.

OTHER BEHAVIOR

Rolling and Crouching

A cat will sometimes roll to one side from a crouched posture to indicate submission when fighting or playing with another cat.

When a cat crouches with its rump on the ground, shaking from side to side, he is getting ready to attack something or someone. Cats often do this when they are playing.

Scratching

Cats scratch not only to sharpen their claws, but also to mark their territory and leave a scent.

Marking

Cats spray urine to mark their territory. Other cats will smell their mark, and recognize that another cat has been there. Both male and female cats spray, although it is more common in males. Neutering a male cat will probably reduce markings, but not stop the cat from spraying completely.

Cats usually meow when they want attention. It's their way of saying, "Hey, I need something."

Gland Markings

In addition to spraying, cats have scent glands that they use to mark certain items or humans. They do this by rubbing the scent glands against them. When a cat is doing this he or she will usually back up to the item or person, and shake her rump against it.

WEEK 13 CHECKLIST

- ✓ Get to know your cat by recognizing different behaviors.
- ✓ Don't stare at your cat — they don't like to hold eye contact.
- ✓ If your cat's behavior is out of control, check for catnip in his toys.

Week 14: Collars & Leashes

Regardless of whether you keep your cat indoors or let her out, I recommend that you put a collar on her, with an identification tag. Even the shyest indoor house cat can escape to the outdoors. If you have an unfamiliar person taking care of your cats while you are away; if you have a guest with a dog who chases your cat; if your cat isn't feeling well and is looking for a place to hole up and hide; all of these situations place stress on kitty and can cause her to slip out a door or window. And by all means, if your kitten is meant to stay indoors but is the adventurous type, you may have a little escape artist on your hands and you want anyone who finds your pet to know where she belongs.

Even the shyest indoor house cat can escape to the outdoors.

COLLARS

I recommend a soft cloth or nylon collar with a breakaway clasp for most cats. The breakaway clasp is a plastic clasp that is made to give way in the event your pet gets caught by the neck on something — shrubbery, a piece of furniture, or a blind or curtain pull. By giving way under such circumstances, this type of collar assures that your kitten won't get strangled. Buckle collars don't offer this built-in safety option. There are a number of different kinds of breakaway clasps, any of which will do.

Your kitten's collar should be loose enough to allow you to put two fingers through it.

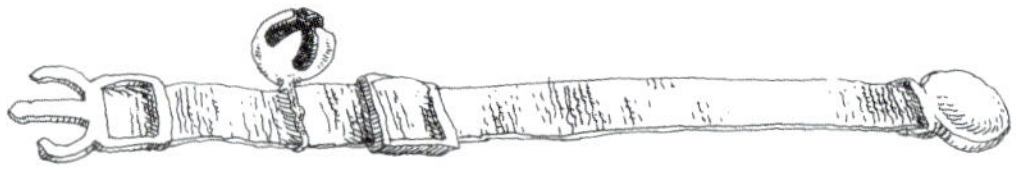

Your kitten's collar should be loose enough to allow you to put two fingers between it and her neck. If it's any looser, kitty might get it caught in her mouth, or put one leg through it. An identification tag with your name, address, and phone number should be attached. I also highly recommend attaching your pet's rabies vaccination tag to the collar. In the event she is picked up by animal control it will be clear to them from the start that she is not a rabies threat. Also, if the I.D. tag ever falls off, your kitten can still be traced through the vet's name and vaccination number on the rabies tag. (It's also a very good idea to keep a current photo of your kitten or cat on hand in case your pet does escape and you have to go looking for her, or want to put up lost-cat flyers.)

Keep an eye on the skin around your kitten's neck under the collar.

COLLAR AND LEASH TIPS

- Put a collar and I.D. tag on your cat even if you keep her indoors.
- Choose a soft collar with a breakaway clasp.
- Make sure the collar is loose enough to allow two fingers in.
- For walking, use a harness and leash.
- Take time to acclimate your cat to a harness before use.
- Keep kitty clean and well-groomed under her collar or harness.

HOW TO WALK A CAT

It's not hard to teach a cat to walk on a leash — it just takes a little time and patience on your part.

- Leave the leash and harness near your cat's favorite spot for a while, a few days or even a week. Let her get used to the look and smell of these items.
- Next, you'll want to put the harness on your pet and let her walk around the house wearing it for a while. After you put it on, give kitty a favorite treat and lots of praise and affection.
- If kitty is visibly upset or displeased with the harness, initiate a play session to take her mind off it. Let her wear the harness until she is relaxed with it on. When she is , attach the leash, and let the kitten drag it around the house for a while, getting used to it. Be sure to supervise these sessions to be sure your pet doesn't get tangled or hung up on something. Repeat over a period of days.
- Next, try actually walking indoors with kitty on the leash. Let her take the lead — you follow. Now you lead, and kitty follows. Use your nicest, sweetest, cajoling tones to encourage your pet to walk with you behind her. If she pulls on the leash so that it gets taut, stop, relax, and gently persuade her to come in your direction. Be sure not to yell or show anger or any abruptness.
- Practice. Don't be discouraged if this takes a while. Keep practicing until your pet is used to walking on the leash indoors before you try it outdoors. Even then, you may just want to go outside and sit with your pet, not going anywhere, until she is acclimated to being outdoors. If she is an indoor cat, she might be a little overwhelmed at first by the sights and sounds of the big world.
- When kitty is relaxed outside, pick up your leash-walking practice where you left off. Do this in a quiet place with as few distractions as possible before you attempt walks in areas with lots of people, dogs, or additional stimulation. Remember, any time your pet shows discomfort, slow down! With determination and continued patience on your part, she will get there.

Be careful to keep this area well groomed and free of mats that can breed skin problems. If your kitten's skin breaks out or even looks irritated, try a collar made of a different material. It's not unusual for cats to have allergies and you don't want your kitten to have a reaction to her collar that will cause any ongoing problems.

LEASHES

Don't laugh! I've known many cat owners who walked their cats. Even if you don't walk your kitty, a leash is a handy thing to have for car travel, especially on any extended trips, when you might want to let your pet out for a potty break. You certainly don't want to let her run loose at a rest area on the interstate.

If you do want to acclimate your cat to walking on a leash, you might want to consider a walking harness. Since cats don't respond to leash commands the way dogs do, there's no particular reason to walk your kitten with a leash that attaches at the collar. A harness may be more comfortable, too, since it doesn't tug at the throat, something that often happens with a cat because they don't walk in the predictable patterns that dogs do. Another advantage of a harness is that your kitten or cat can't pull out of it, something that is fairly easy for a determined cat to do with a collar. That's the last thing you need in the middle of a walk, especially when you are just beginning to acclimate your kitten to a leash. You will just have to make a judgment based on your individual cat.

I recommend against retractable leashes for both cats and dogs. They may be useful in training your pet in the comfort of your own home or yard, but when you are out walking an animal in public places, they don't give you enough control over the animal's movements. Aside from that, any sturdy nylon leash will do.

WEEK 14 CHECKLIST

- ✓ Make sure your kitten has a collar that will stay on, and one that will be safe.
- ✓ Look into getting a leash for your cat – especially if he's an indoor-only kitty. This will be a safe way for you to take him outside on occasion.
- ✓ Learn how to walk your cat – and do it regularly.

Week 15: Cats & Birds

Let it be said that cats and birds have been adversaries from time immemorial and nothing you do will ever change that. If you let your cat outside, chances are he is going to hunt birds to some degree or another. The instinct to hunt varies from one cat to another; people who have two outdoor cats often report that one brings little gifts of prey home every day while the other seems to have no interest in catching anything other than a nap.

That said, there are a few things you can do to address the issue of Your Cat vs. The Neighborhood Birds, whether it is in the interest of your own garden birds or neighbor relations.

CAT PROOFING TRICKS

If you choose to let your kitten, soon to be a cat, outdoors, it really isn't fair to also have birdhouses or feeders. I strongly recommend that, before you get your kitten, you make a choice between attracting birds to your yard or having an outdoor cat. Even if you do not attract birds to

I strongly recommend that, before you get your kitten, you make a choice between attracting birds to your yard or having an outdoor cat.

your property, you may still be faced with a cat who stalks the neighbors' feeders. In this case, for the sake of keeping the peace, you can choose from several, if not all, of the following courses of action.

SAVING THE BIRDS

- Do not encourage birds into your yard if you let your kitten outdoors.
- Plant prickly plants and shrubs around bird-feeding stations.
- Try a deterrent around the trunks of trees where birds nest.
- Bell your cat.
- Keep your cat fed well on a healthy and satisfying diet. Ideally, don't let your kitten outside!

Plant anything prickly

Plants with prickles and thorns growing around bird-feeding stations and shelters will deter cats to some extent from these areas. If you insist on maintaining bird attraction sites in your own yard, you can certainly plant species that fit this description, such as pyracantha, rose bushes, berries such as blackberries or raspberries, blackthorn, or hawthorn.

Don't even think about trying to erect a physical barrier such as a wall or a fence. Cats are expert climbers and love a challenge. You'll be wasting your time and money.

Tree barriers

Birds in nests are like a drug to many outdoor cats and climbing a tree to get at them is just what cats love to do best. It is difficult to keep a natural-born tree-climbing cat from doing what it most loves to

do, but all is not lost.

You can try tying branches of a prickly plant or shrub around the trunk of the tree.

Or, check with your local pet store for a belt-like device with spikes on it that can be strapped around the trunk to keep cats from climbing past it.

TO BELL OR NOT TO BELL

Many people attach a bell to their cat's collar to help reduce their rate of hunting success. It is debatable whether a bell actually prevents a cat from catching a bird. While your neighbors who could potentially complain about your bird-hunting kitten might feel better once you attach the bell, birds are not likely to hear it ring until it is too late. This is because cats hunt by waiting patiently and remaining absolutely still for long periods of time before pouncing rapidly on their prey. By the time the bird hears your cat's bell, it will probably just be the last thing it hears.

FOOD AS PREVENTION

If you're worried about the birds, it can't hurt to make sure that your cat is getting a healthy, nutritious diet and has enough to eat. A well-fed cat is less likely to hunt — but won't necessarily totally refrain from hunting. Still, having plenty to eat is at least a partial deterrent.

The only completely effective deterrent is to keep your cat indoors, or at least keep time outside to a minimum.

WEEK 15 CHECKLIST

- ✓ Decide if you will continue to attract birds to your yard now that you have a cat.
- ✓ If birds have already made themselves at home in your yard, kitten-proof their sanctuaries.
- ✓ Decide whether or not you should bell your cat.

Week 16: Cats & Cars

I hear and see enough horror stories about cats and cars in my practice to believe it is a good idea to dedicate this week's chapter to the subject. Generally speaking, cats and cars don't mix. Most cats don't like riding in cars unless they have been exposed to them from a very early age. Even if cats aren't afraid of cars, inappropriate car cat care on the part of the owner can still lead to serious injury or death. At this stage of your kitty's life, let's stop and review some important considerations with regard to your car. With a few simple precautions you will have nothing to worry about.

KEEP YOUR CAT INDOORS

You're going to hear me saying this again and again in this book, but the best way to keep your cat safe from cars and all the other dangers of the outside world is to keep him indoors. If you could stand in my shoes and see the kitties that come into my clinic after being hit by cars, you wouldn't consider letting your cat outside for even one minute. Even if you live in the middle of nowhere, it only takes a fraction of a second for a cat to be in the wrong place at the wrong time. And when a cat has her eye on a bird, a squirrel, another cat, or any other destination of interest, she isn't going to stop and look both ways before crossing the road.

You should know that antifreeze is a deadly poison. One teaspoonful is all it takes to fatally poison a cat.

What's worse is that cats are typically not killed instantly when they are hit by cars. Their strong athletic little bodies are able to carry them quickly under the wheels, where they are damaged in ways that are heartbreaking to see.

Another one I frequently hear is "My cat knows to stay out of the road." Baloney! It's just not possible to teach cats this sort of thing. They aren't thinking about the dangers of road traffic any more than they are debating the ingredients for a chocolate souffle. If you choose to let your kitten become an outdoor cat, know now that you are taking your pet's life in your hands.

CAT & CAR SAFETY

- Keep your cat indoors if possible.
- Store antifreeze in cat-safe areas.
- Beware of puddles of leaked antifreeze in driveway or garage.
- Knock on your car hood before starting your car.
- Get your kitten used to the car before he associates it strictly with vet visits.
- Keep a window cracked while traveling.

BEWARE THE GARAGE AND DRIVEWAY

Setting the roadway traffic issue aside, there are plenty of other car-related dangers to your kitten. These are much easier to mitigate, because they all involve factors that are more or less within your control.

You should know that antifreeze is a deadly poison. One teaspoonful is all it takes to fatally poison a cat. Keep antifreeze tightly capped and stored in a place your kitten can't get to. Just as important, be careful in the garage. Cars often leak antifreeze, and if you keep your cat in the garage or let her into the garage or onto the driveway, she may be attracted to the puddle. Keep such spots cleaned up!

Make it a habit, when you go out to start your car, to knock on the hood and fenders of your vehicle. Especially in cold weather, outdoor cats will search out the warmth of a car engine and will quite commonly climb up into the engine to curl up and sleep. Or, your cat could climb up onto one of your car's tires. The simple act of starting the car's engine could be enough to seriously injure or even kill a kitten or cat, and it certainly won't do your car any favors either.

TRAVEL SAFELY

I recommend taking your cat for a ride in the car now and then, when you are going somewhere other than the vet's office. Cats are smart little animals, and they will

otherwise learn very quickly that when you get out the cat carrier and, even worse, load kitty and carrier into the car, that it means a trip to the dreaded clinic. Then every time you take your cat to the clinic you will have a fight on your hands, or at best a game of hide-and-seek.

Put your kitten in his carrier now and then and just take him out to the parked car. Give him a treat and lots of petting and praise, then carry him back into the house. Gradually you can work up to short trips.

Always keep your kitten in a carrier during car travel. The kitten will feel much more secure when confined. And, in case of an accident, she will be protected. If she is loose in the car she could even cause an accident by jumping on

THE VET'S NOTEBOOK

Cats and Cars

One of my first cases when training to be a vet was treating a cat who had crawled up into the engine of a car to get warm. That certainly was not my last or only case, but is probably the most memorable.

This cat had a habit of crawling into the owner's engine, and the owner would usually knock on the hood or give some warning to the cat to get out before starting the car. She was in a hurry one day and didn't give the warning signs, and it almost cost her the cat's life. She actually didn't find out about this accident for a few days.

The cat had been missing for about three days, and the owners had searched everywhere. On the fourth day, the cat finally showed up, and it was real sick. It had apparently been hit by the fan in the engine of the car, and was pretty mangled. After he was injured in the car, he was apparently so traumatized that he was afraid to go back home to the scene of the accident.

All of the hair had been stripped off of his rear and tail. The skin had gotten infected from going so long without being treated. He also had a broken hip and lots of other lacerations.

As it turns out, this cat was very lucky, because we were able to save him. I don't see many of these cases where the cat can be saved.

So, if you have an outdoor cat and park your car outdoors, or have an indoor cat that has access to your car in your garage, take that extra second or two to make sure the cat is not in the engine.

you while you are driving or getting in between your foot and the brake pedal.

Make sure you crack a window while driving to give kitty some fresh air. This will help prevent carsickness, overheating, and dehydration. Don't make the mistake of thinking that it's okay to leave kitty in the parked car for any length of time at any time of year as long as the window is open. Even in cool weather, the sun will heat your car up quickly and could cause heat stroke, dehydration, or even death.

On trips of any length you might consider bringing along some familiar toys or bedding to help kitty feel more comfortable and at home. A traumatized cat can become dehydrated and ill and you want your kitten to feel as relaxed as possible. It's ideal to have at least one passenger with you who can keep an eye on your kitten and be available to comfort it if necessary.

For more tips on traveling with your cat, refer to Week 20.

WEEK 16 CHECKLIST

- ✓ Be aware of all the hazards cars pose to cats.
- ✓ Protect your cat from cars – on the road, in the driveway, and in the garage.
- ✓ Clean any fluids leaking from your car that could be hazardous to your cat.
- ✓ Get your cat used to riding in the car – and not just when going to the vet.

Notes:

Notes:

Week 17: To Have — or Not Have — Kittens

If you have a female cat and think you might want her to have kittens, now is the time to give serious consideration to that decision.

BREEDING ISSUES

If your pet is a purebred that is an excellent physical example of her breed, has an exemplary temperament for her breed, or has a unique or desirable color or any other hard-to-find characteristic, breeding your kitten might be something you want to consider. But let me be emphatic: these are really the only reasons to consider having kittens, and even then I would think very carefully about the responsibility you incur by adding new kittens to this overpopulated world, before you take this step.

The technical aspects of breeding (how to find a suitable mate or how

to properly care for a new mother and a litter of kittens, for example) are far too broad a topic to cover in this book. I often counsel cat owners who are considering breeding their kittens, and I urge you to talk to your veterinarian about it. You can also get information from clubs and other breeder organizations, go to the library, or hop on the Internet.

In any event, breeding is not a decision to be rushed into. I strongly recommend that you postpone any final decision on the issue for as long as it takes to be certain that your kitten has no congenital problems.

Even if all the other criteria for breeding (appearance, temperament, rare or desirable characteristics) are present, would you breed your cat knowing that a congenital abnormality is being passed on to another generation of kittens — and contributing to the deterioration of the breed?

As I've said before, backyard breeding is one of the major contributing factors in the deterioration of popular breeds.

By far the most common circumstance in which backyard breeding occurs is when two friends own a male and female of the same (or very similar) breed, and decide to mate their cats. Far more commonly, people who have cats often just think it would be cute or fun to have a litter of little baby kittens in the house. Or this is how they rationalize delaying the decision to spay, anyway. Then, when kittens arrive, the reality hits.

There are too many cats already in the world. Even if you give them away free, kittens are difficult to place in good homes. More often than not, they end up at a shelter where resources are already overloaded by well-intentioned (or

PROS AND CONS OF BREEDING

PROS:

- Sometimes breeding will change the temperament of a female cat, making her more affectionate and laid back.
- If you have a healthy, well-formed, mature, well-behaved, good-natured, purebred cat, you can pass these traits on to another generation.

CONS:

- Medical evidence suggests that your cat is less likely to develop health problems (such as an enlarged prostate) if he or she is neutered or spayed before reaching maturity. Delaying this to breed may compromise your cat's health.
- According to the Humane Society of the U.S., one out of every four animals found in shelters each year is purebred. You'll be adding to this problem by breeding.
- A cat that has been sterilized is usually better behaved than on that has not.
- Each litter of kittens that is born contributes to the massive animal overpopulation in our country. Even if you find a home for every kitten, that will be one less animal that will be rescued from a shelter or picked up off the street.

otherwise) people who thought it might be fun to have kittens.

Examine your motives

If you do have an exceptional feline and after careful thought you decide to breed your kitten, ask yourself the following additional questions. What will you do with the kittens when they are old enough to leave the litter? If you plan to sell them, what will you do with any unsold kittens? Is your decision to breed your cat based solely on the immediate desires of you and your family?

Consider the fact that three million to four million unwanted animals are euthanized each year.

As you ponder these questions, you should also consider the fact that three to four million unwanted animals are euthanized each year, according to the Humane Society of the United States.

WEEK 17 CHECKLIST

- ✓ Decide whether or not you will breed your cat. For most people, the answer to this should be No!
- ✓ If you think you may want to breed your kitten, be sure to do lots of research — this usually turns out to be a bad idea.
- ✓ Examine your motives for breeding carefully — consider that three to four million unwanted animals are euthanized each year.

Week 18: Troubleshooting Problem Behaviors

Cats are not small dogs. They cannot be expected to learn or even listen to commands. Unfortunately, like dogs, they misbehave just as frequently. When that happens, yelling, screaming, or physically abusing your kitten are the wrong things to do. For one thing, they won't have the desired effect. If anything, loud or violent reprimands will only confuse your pet and could make her afraid of you. There are other ways to effect changes in your kitten's problem behaviors; most of them have to do with tricking the kitty into teaching herself what to do and what not to do. Here are a few tips.

ARE YOU THE PROBLEM?

Before leaping to the conclusion that your kitten has a problem, take a look at your own behavior. People tend to believe that cats are an aloof species who need little if anything from humans. Nothing could be farther from the truth. Your kitten depends on you for attention, affection, food, and shelter. She looks to you for fun, comfort, exercise, and security — in short, for everything.

If your kitten is acting out in any way, it could be because you are not giving her some of the basics, or enough of the basics, that she needs to thrive. Be sure you take time out of every day to play with her. Give her toys and offer opportunities and outlets for her high spirits and energy. If you can't spend time with your kitten or find a way to make an effort to give her what she needs, you probably don't need to be the owner of a kitten and should consider a pet that makes fewer demands on your attention.

CHEWING

Lots of cat owners complain about their pets chewing or licking things: the corners of books or magazines, chair legs, electrical cords, shoes, even human toes and fingers. Rest assured that this is normal and natural behavior,

Be sure your kitty has plenty of toys to play with.

especially for a young kitten. Make sure you have kitten-proofed your home as described in Week 5. Once that is taken care of, you'll need to be sure your kitty has plenty of toys to play with, and enough play time with you to work some of that energy out of her system.

BEHAVIOR-CONTROL TIPS

- Use pepper sprays and other bad-tasting deterrents to prevent unwanted licking, chewing, nibbling, or clawing.
- Make sure you have a scratching post or cat tree and encourage kitty to use it.
- Stop interaction when kitty misbehaves.
- When a cat misbehaves, yelling, screaming, or physically abusing him won't help.
- Use timeouts.
- Give kitty plenty of toys, attention, affection, and personal interaction time.
- If your cat's behavior is out of control, check to be sure his toys don't have catnip in them.
- Consult your vet if serious misbehavior continues — your kitten might be telling you he doesn't feel well.

This doesn't mean you have to go to the store and buy a lot of stuff. Kittens love to play with crumpled up balls of paper or empty toilet paper rolls; more than anything, they love to play with anything that YOU throw or dangle in front of them during playtime.

As far as electrical wires go, if your kitten is still getting to them in spite of your kitty-proofing efforts, you can try spraying them with bitter apple or pepper spray (from your local pet store), both of which kitties hate. Tabasco sauce is another deterrent for anything you don't want your cat to put her mouth on. If you can catch kitty in the act, it's useful to have a can full of coins around that you shake to startle her when she starts her chewing. With some creativity, you could even booby-trap the area to cause the can to topple when you aren't around. Cats hate unexpected loud noises; a few shakes of your coin can should teach her that touching those cords is not a fun experience. You might also try putting double-sided tape on the floor near the cords she is bothering. She will have to step on the tape to get to the cords and won't like the sticky feel on her feet.

Tabasco sauce is another deterrent for anything you don't want your cat to put her mouth on.

SCRATCHING AND CLAWING

If your kitten is scratching and clawing at furniture, the first thing to do is make sure she has a scratching post, and encourage her to use it. You can at the same time

discourage her from using the furniture by putting some bitter apple, cayenne pepper or pepper spray, or tabasco on the spots where she is clawing (test this first to make sure the fabric doesn't stain).

Encourage kitty to use the scratching post by putting some treats and favorite toys nearby, and by praising and treating her when you see her using it. One trick a lot of cat owners use for discouraging any form of unwanted behavior is to keep a spray water bottle handy and squirt kitty when she misbehaves. This sometimes works and sometimes doesn't. Some cats actually get used to the water and decide they like it!

If your kitten is biting, scratching, or clawing at you, the trick is to immediately stop all interaction with her.

If your kitten is biting, scratching, or clawing at you, the trick is to immediately stop all interaction with her. Do not continue your play or petting or whatever you are doing. She will learn fairly quickly that these behaviors lead to being ignored.

If scratching, clawing, and biting behaviors are part of an overall aggressive acting-out problem, I suggest giving your pet a short timeout to calm down. Put him or her in the bathroom or another small, dark, quiet room for 10 or 15 minutes when this sort of thing happens. Repeat as often as needed.

JUMPING UP

It is difficult if not impossible to keep a kitten from exploring your house, especially when you are not there. Cats are by nature curious and there's nothing you can do about that. But you can take a few measures to discourage jumping on countertops and other unwanted places.

Your local pet store will sell various repellent sprays that you can use; although if kitty is getting on the kitchen counters you may not want to spray this stuff all over. It won't hurt you, but just requires a certain amount of cleanup. You might try placing a piece of thin cardboard across the counter and leaving it hanging off the edge.

Place a can of coins on the far end of the cardboard nearest the wall. When kitty jumps up the cardboard will come down, flinging the coins up into the air and down — all of which will be very noisy, a totally unpleasant surprise for kitty.

You can also try putting aluminum foil on your counters; cats hate foil and will avoid it.

I'd also suggest that you look into purchasing a cat tree. This is a covered pole with sitting platforms where kitties can get up high and perch, which they enjoy doing enormously. Don't keep food on your kitchen counters, as that is probably what your cat or kitten is trying to reach by jumping up there.

If your cat is jumping on you, try making an unexpected loud noise or clapping your hands or both when she does this. She won't like it and after a few times will realize that she is not getting the result she wanted!

EATING PLANTS

This is a common problem. Whether kitty is digging in the dirt or eating the leaves you don't want her damaging your house plants or making herself sick. A couple of things work pretty well.

Try spraying plant leaves with cayenne pepper spray.

Try spraying plant leaves with cayenne pepper spray or sprinkling cayenne pepper right on the leaves. You can buy the spray at a pet store or make it yourself using powdered cayenne and water.

I also suggest putting aluminum foil on top of the dirt in the pot. Cats don't like the feel of foil and usually leave it alone. You can also use plastic or stones on top of the dirt.

As with some of the other misbehaviors we've discussed here, you can also make a loud, unpleasant, unexpected noise when your cat starts chewing on plants. Clap your hands, screech, or make a sound that she doesn't expect and she will begin to associate the unpleasant loud sound with the plant leaves.

Another technique is to simply remove the problem plant to a part of the house where kitty can't get to it. Leave it there for a time, then move it back to its original spot. If kitty bothers it, move it again. Eventually kitty will get over her fascination for this particular plant.

GOING OUTSIDE THE LITTER BOX

If your kitten is consistently "missing" the box with his urination or defecation, he is trying to tell you something. Your kitten has either a health problem or there is something about the box he doesn't like.

Are you keeping the box impeccably clean? Many cats refuse to use litter boxes that are soiled.

You should try switching types of litter. Many cats have preferences or dislikes; and it's possible that your kitten has an allergy to your litter, particularly if it is the kind that has deodorizing or scented crystals in it. Try using a plain clay litter.

If you have two felines in the house, you should have a litter box for each cat. Many animals will not share a litter box with another pet

and will show their disapproval by going outside the box.

If you've done all of the above and your cat is still "going" in the wrong places, consult your vet. There may be a health problem involved and your kitty is just trying to tell you she doesn't feel good in the best way that she can.

HUNTING

Cats are natural hunters and there's nothing you can do to change that, aside from keeping kitty indoors. The shorthaired American and British cats are the best hunters; if you own this type of kitten you no doubt have a hunter on your hands.

If you choose to let kitty outside you can bell her, but as discussed in Week 15, this probably won't make much of a difference.

The only thing you really can control, if you are letting kitty outside, is the way you dispose of her kill. Please keep in mind that the small game kitty brings home can be full of all kinds of parasites and diseases. Be sure to don rubber gloves before disposing of these creatures and wash your hands thoroughly with soap and hot water afterward.

WEEK 18 CHECKLIST

- ✓ Do not yell at your cat for doing something wrong – this will only add to the problem.
- ✓ Make sure you aren't the problem – spending quality time with your cat each day will help him be well adjusted and happy.
- ✓ Be sure your kitty has plenty of toys so he isn't as tempted to destroy your home for entertainment.
- ✓ Use sprays and repellents to keep your cat out of places he shouldn't be.
- ✓ If your kitty isn't using the litter box properly, talk to your vet about some possible solutions.

Week 19: Lost Cats

It has been said that cats know their place, but a kitten's compass can get thrown off every now and then, particularly a young, indoor cat who winds up outside in unfamiliar territory. In general, a cat will not roam unless he is looking for a mating partner. Instead, a cat prefers to stay home and defend his territory. That said, if your cat gets lost, take steps immediately to find him.

CATS DON'T GO FAR

Chances are your cat is closer than you'd expect, and just as eager for your reunion as you are. With that in mind, start out by looking in the immediate area of your house.

Be sure to check under bushes, in holes, under porches, and in any exterior entrances to your house or houses nearby. Check sewage drains, basements, and other hiding places where a cat could get stuck Don't just stand by the bush or other hiding places and call your cat, but actually look by moving the branches on the bush and scanning the area underneath. A flashlight is usually helpful, even during the day. Your cat may be hidden in the dark corners under your deck. It is not unusual for a cat to be hidden and not respond to your calls.

Especially common for indoor-only cats who have somehow gotten out is to go into "scaredy cat" mode. This is a protective "trance"

I have heard of cases where cats have been found very close to their house, hiding under a bush, several days after going missing.

where they are so scared that they won't respond to your voice. I have heard of cases where cats have been found very close to their house, hiding under a bush, several days after going missing. It's your job to find the cat and somehow coax her out of hiding with food, or just grab her if you can reach her.

If you don't find your cat around your house, you'll have to move out to areas further from your home. It is best to do this on foot as far as possible, because your cat can pick up your scent if you are moving around on foot but not if you are traveling by car. Second, call out to your cat in the same voice you use to speak to him at home. If he is nearby and scared, the familiar sound of your voice will reassure him. Listen very closely for your cat to reply. Carry a container of his favorite treat, and shake the canister to make lots of noise with it. If the treat doesn't make a noise, carry an opened can of tuna or other food that he can readily smell. This may bring a cat out of hiding even when your voice doesn't.

STILL MISSING

If this doesn't produce your kitty, print some LOST CAT flyers and post as many as you can within a one-mile radius of your home. Also, ask your neighbors if they have seen your cat, and ask them to call you if they see him in the future. If you have neighbors who aren't home, leave a flier on their front door.

PROTECT YOUR CAT NOW

Protect your cat now before he or she is lost.

- Pet-proof your house and yard to ensure your cat's containment.

TIPS FOR FINDING A LOST CAT

- Cats don't usually go far, so start near your home.
- Look closely in all possible hiding places, including under bushes, cars, and porches, as well as in holes, sewage drains, and basements.
- Don't count on your pet to come when you call.
- Carry some food for the cat to smell. A smelly can of tuna should work well.
- Hand out flyers and post as many as possible in a 1-mile radius of your home.
- Call your local humane society and your local animal-control authority to see if they have your cat.
- Don't panic. If you don't find your cat right away, she will probably show up when she gets hungry.

- Keep your cat in the house at all times. I say this repeatedly throughout the book, but it's the safest route.
- Always transport your kitty in a carrier. If you try to carry your cat to and from the car, she is likely to be frightened by loud noises and bolt out of your arms. She can also jump out of the car while you are opening or closing the door.
- Get some good photos of your pet now, before it's too late. Take several photos until you get one that really is a good likeness of your kitty. This can be invaluable to put on flyers if your cat becomes lost.
- Ensure that YOU can be located if your pet is found.
- Always keep a collar on your pet with a tag that has your CURRENT PHONE NUMBER on it.
- Always have a CURRENT rabies tag attached to your cat's collar.
- Spay or neuter your cat. Both males and females will be much less likely to roam if they are spayed or neutered.
- If you move, keep your cat indoors for at least three weeks

before letting it go outside (if you have an outdoors cat). Supervise its initial outdoor jaunts.

A TECHNOLOGICAL APPROACH

While looking for your cat close to home and putting flyers out usually produces your lost cat, there are some ways you can be sure your cat will be identified if found far from home.

Microchip implant

This is a fail-safe way to ensure that your cat can be identified and that the finder will know who to contact. Most shelters scan animals for this ID device. Talk to your vet and some local shelters about which brand of chip is most prevalent in your area. They can probably give you contact information for the company that makes them.

Tattoo

Tattoos aren't as reliable for identification as a microchip, because they can be difficult to read. Hair will grow over them, and it's sometimes hard to get a frightened cat to be still to look for this brand. I have found that the best place to apply a tattoo is on the inner thigh. Pet thieves have been known to cut off a tattooed ear!

WEEK 19 CHECKLIST

- ✓ Take measures to ensure that your cat won't get lost.
- ✓ Keep your cat in the house at all times.
- ✓ Make sure he has a collar with your current contact information.
- ✓ Get a good photo of your cat in case he becomes lost.
- ✓ Consider getting a microchip implant or tattoo for your cat. This helps ensure that he will be returned to you if found by someone else.

Week 20: Cats & Vacations

Getting ready to go on vacation or preparing for a business trip? You have several options for what to do with your new pet. You can leave her at home, board her, or take her with you.

LEAVING YOUR KITTEN HOME

If you have a friend or family member who could take her into their home for a short time, this may work, but cats are usually happier just hanging out in their own space, even if you're not there.

I recommend leaving the kitten at home, and having a friend or neighbor check on him once a day or so. They can make sure he has food and water, and play with him for a few minutes so he doesn't feel so lonely.

BOARDING

If you board your kitty, you may want to leave her food for her to eat while there. Sudden changes in diet can cause digestive problems, which can in turn lead to serious problems with vomiting or diarrhea.

If your cat is on any kind of medication prescribed by your vet, the meds certainly should be left for the boarding facility to administer. You might also check to see if the facility permits toys to be brought from home.

Always be sure your boarding facility knows how to reach you, 24 hours a day, in case of emergency. A cell phone number works best.

TRAVELING WITH YOUR KITTEN

The primary "pro" to having your kitty accompany you on a long trip is the satisfaction of not being separated from a beloved family member. That aside, you need to carefully consider all of the issues involved in traveling with a kitty before you head off on some lengthy trek.

I do not recommend traveling with a kitten less than four months old.

First of all, I do not recommend traveling with a kitten less than four months old. The first several weeks at home with the family is a critical time in a cat's development, a time when you are building a bond of trust between you and your pet. Taking the kitten out of an environment where he is still learning to feel safe can damage that trust.

Another reason for waiting until your kitty is a little older before taking him on the road is the possibility of disease transmission.

BOARDING YOUR CAT

Ideally, if you have to leave town, your cat will be able to stay in a familiar environment, either at home with a pet sitter or at a friend's home where she will be comfortable, but this isn't always possible.

If you need to board your cat you should be careful about choosing your boarding facility. Ask your vet if they offer boarding services, or ask them for a recommendation on a facility nearby.

You should make every effort to walk through the boarding facility before dropping your cat off. Is it clean? Do all of the cats have clean water, food, and litter boxes?

Ask the staff how often the animals' cages are cleaned, how many employees there are at any given time to care for the animals, and (if the boarding facility isn't part of your animal clinic) what vet they use if any of the animals have a medical problem.

TRAVEL TIPS

- Get your cat used to traveling short distances before you take her on long trips.
- Drive short distances that don't end in a vet visit.
- Acclimate your cat to a leash and harness if you will need to walk her during the trip.
- Always keep your cat in the carrier while driving.
- Check with any hotels or resorts on their animal policy before making reservations.
- You may need a health certificate for your pet to allow them to cross some state lines or to board an airplane.
- Always be sure that your cat is getting plenty of food, water, and time with a litter box while you travel.

This possibility exists any time your cat is in contact with other animals, and the chances go up when traveling. In particular, campgrounds and RV parks (public parks in general, for that matter) are areas where individuals from various backgrounds and with varying pet care practices congregate with their animals. It only takes one diseased animal to contaminate an entire area, so I would avoid this type of exposure until your kitty's immune system is strong enough to handle these riskier environments.

Avoid campgrounds and RV parks until your kitty's immune system is strong enough to handle it.

Car sickness is another consideration for traveling with your pet. Cats are susceptible to varying degrees of car sickness. The first line of defense in dealing with this problem is not allowing your kitty to eat a large meal for a few hours prior to leaving on the trip — although a small amount of food on the stomach (no more than a few

bites) may actually be helpful in keeping the stomach settled and the kitty calm. Your veterinarian may prescribe a tranquilizing medication to calm the kitty and prevent vomiting.

Earlier in this book, I talked about the safety advantages of using a carrier when transporting your cat by car, and of securing the carrier while in the car. This applies to long trips as well as short. When traveling with your cat, confirm in advance that the place you plan to stay accepts and accommodates pets. If you're staying with friends, this is just common courtesy.

Many hotels and resorts allow pets of a certain size, but you won't know for sure unless you ask. When traveling to other states or countries, a health certificate is usually required by law, with significant fines possible if you cannot produce your kitty's certificate on demand.

When traveling with your cat, confirm in advance that the place you plan to stay accepts and accommodates pets.

Health certification is also generally required for plane travel, and other restrictions on traveling with animals may also apply, depending on factors ranging from weather conditions to individual airline policies and regulations. If you want to travel by air with your cat, plan well in advance to avoid having to leave her behind at the airport. Most airlines can give you details about traveling with pets.

WEEK 20 CHECKLIST

- ✓ Decide what you will do with your kitty when you have to travel.
- ✓ If you will board your kitty, investigate the boarding facility beforehand.
- ✓ If you leave your kitten at home, be sure someone can check on him at least once a day to make sure he has food and water, and that he hasn't gotten into something dangerous.
- ✓ If traveling with your kitten, avoid campgrounds and RV parks until his immune system strong enough to handle the hazards.
- ✓ Confirm in advance that the place you are travelling to accommodates pets.

Notes:

Notes:

Week 21: Frequently Asked Questions

Q: *My cat sometimes opens his mouth and seems to pant. Is he okay?*

A: Cats smell not only with their noses, but also with something called their "Jacobson's organ" which is located on the surface of the mouth. If a cat is concentrating on identifying a scent he may open his mouth to "sample" the air.

If your cat is actually panting, however, and continues to do this for any length of time, then there may be a problem.

Some cats pant when they are in pain, but the most likely reason is that he is overheated. Cats become overheated easily; it only take a few minutes in a hot car without proper ventilation. Whatever is going on with your cat, panting requires immediate attention.

Q: *Is it okay for me to have my groomer cut my cat's whiskers?*

A: Cats can squeeze through any space large enough for their head. This is one of the important functions of whiskers: you will sometimes see a cat testing an opening by sticking his head in and seeing if his whiskers touch the edges. The loss of the whiskers takes away one of the cat's tools that he uses to explore his environment.

Q: *My cat is always getting up in the middle of the night to play. How can I get him to sleep through the night?*

A: Cats sleep an average of 16-18 hours per day, but these are not necessarily consecutive hours. There's a reason we call very short naps "cat naps!" If your cat is alone for large parts of the day, then he's probably getting a lot of sleeping done then. If you move "play time" to late in the evening, taking this time to play with your cat and use up some of his energy, then he's more likely to sleep soundly through the night.

Q: *Are all white cats deaf?*

A: Most white cats with blue eyes are deaf, yes. If a white cat has one blue eye, the ear closest to this eye is most likely deaf. White cats with any other color eyes are usually free of this handicap. Deaf cats, however, can make wonderful pets as long as they aren't let outside. Since they are unable to hear a car or other threat coming, the outdoors is much more dangerous for a deaf cat.

Q: *My cat doesn't seem to respond to catnip. What does this mean?*

A: Nothing. Approximately 20% of cats simply have no reaction to the herb. There's nothing wrong with this, it's just a different reaction that's linked to genetics.

Q: *I adopted my cat and have since developed an allergy to her. Do I have to get rid of her?*

A: Not necessarily. Many people with mild to moderate allergies to animals still keep pets. Your vet or groomer may be able to recommend a special shampoo for your cat that will reduce the allergens in her coat. Cleanliness is also essential. The more you comb and clean your cat, the less opportunity her coat will have to produce dander, which is most likely the element of the cat that you are allergic to. Vacuuming up cat hair and dander, and maybe getting an air purifier, will also lower the amount of particles in your home. If you establish a "no cat zone," usually your bedroom, then you'll have an easier time keeping the dander under control. Keeping your bedroom dander-free will also keep you from lying awake trying to breathe.

Allergy shots are also a possibility, so see your doctor. There is at least one drug, which is in the final stages of development, designed specifically for this allergy. Ask your doctor for details about these medical options.

Q: *I'm about to move. What can I do to make the transition easier for my cat?*

A: Cats are territorial animals, so they won't be happy to leave their "turf" under any circumstances. There are a few things that you can do to make the transition easier, though. First of all, keep your cat close to home for a while before the move. Many cats have ended up being left behind because the packing and the moving men scared them, they hid, and the family couldn't find them in time. Be sure to take your cat's toys, bed, blanket, and scratching post with you. Once you arrive you may want to pick a small room, such as a bathroom, and shut the cat, with food, water, and the familiar objects, in the room while furniture and boxes are being carried in and out. If your cat has been an indoor-outdoor cat up to this point, then he will need to become a strictly indoor animal for at least two weeks after the move. This gives him the time to associate the new residence with you and the food and affection that you provide. If he is let out before this association is made then he is likely to wander off looking for his old territory. If you have been thinking about making your cat into a strictly indoor cat then this would be an ideal opportunity to make the transition. Just a little extra care and attention to your pet during this confusing and disorienting time will go a long way toward making the experience easier for everyone involved.

Q: *My cat fights with my other cats and dogs. What can I do?*

A: There is always a reason behind aggressive behavior, and finding the source of the aggression is the key to stopping it. It may be something as obvious as your cat feeling intimidated by the larger dog, or as subtle as one of the other cats challenging the dominant cat for position. There are several hormonal reasons behind aggression that may affect an unsterilized cat. If your cat is unneutered, and if you don't intend to breed him at any point, then having him neutered (or spayed if female) may remove the motivation for fighting. See the Hormone-Related Aggression box on page 155 and also the box on hierarchy in a multiple cat home on page 51.

Q: *My cat is a picky eater! How can I get him to eat his food?*

A: There are several reasons that cause a cat to turn up his nose at his food. First, check to make sure that there isn't a medical problem that's causing his appetite to diminish. Then check that the local rodent population isn't being reduced. If he's been eating a steady diet of mouse then he isn't picky, he's just full! If neither of these reasons appear to be behind the hunger strike, then make sure you've chosen a high quality food, preferably dry or semi-moist, and offer it to your cat. If it isn't eaten, offer it again the next day, and the next until the cat gets hungry enough to eat it. Remain consistent. Don't change your cat's food often and don't feed him table scraps to try to tempt him. These things only make the problem worse. As a last resort, look at your cat's bowl. Some plastic bowls have been known to cause sores in cats' mouths, and some metal bowls can deliver a static shock in the wintertime. Ceramic or glass bowls are best, if you suspect that these are the problem. If nothing works, see your vet again. There may be an undetected health problem.

Q: *My cat is jumping on the counters and on my car and I cannot get her to stop. Are there any tricks that can keep my cat off of these areas?*

A: Cats are natural jumpers. They also naturally love high places where they can survey their domain with ease. This is one of those natural instincts that should be redirected rather than eliminated. Perhaps you could designate a few high places that your cat is allowed to jump onto. The washer and dryer, a bookshelf, or a piece of cat furniture might work. To encourage your cat to use these places, hide food treats every few days in the spots that you want to encourage her to use. When she jumps to these places, praise her with attention and love. When she tries to jump onto counters or your car, block her way and give a verbal command such as "NO" or "OFF!" If she gets off immediately, praise her or give her a treat. Positive reinforcement is the key. When you aren't there to discourage her from using the forbidden places, you can either booby trap them or isolate her from them. Close the cat (with food, water, and litter box) in a room without boundaries until you return, or you can "booby trap" the counters and other surfaces. Place double-sided tape on the counters (around the edges and at spots along the counter, perhaps) which your cat won't like to step on. If this doesn't work, you can try popping a balloon in your cat's presence, then taping balloons on these areas. You may even go so far as to build a pyramid of empty cans, then attach a string, with a treat or toy on the end of it, to the bottom can. When your cat pulls the string the cans will fall off the counter, and the cat will associate the counters with this frightening experience. These are very strong teaching experiences because the cat associates the environment with the punishment rather than you. You will not lose your cat's trust and the point will still be taken. Always remember that negative reinforcement, such as yelling, chasing, or spraying your cat, damages your cat's trust in you more than her desire to jump on the counters or car. Positive reinforcement is the key.

Q. *Are calico cats always female?*

A. Calico and related colors are the result of a sex-linked gene and require two X chromosomes to appear. Generally speaking, these colors will appear only in females. Very rarely, these colors may appear in male cats, but these males are genetically abnormal (they have XXY instead of the normal XY) and are almost always infertile.

Q. *I have a cat who goes indoors and outdoors. How can I ensure that she can get in when she needs to if I'm not at home?*

A. If you have decided to let your cat be an indoor-outdoor cat, a pet door can be a big convenience for both you and your pet. There are several types of pet doors out there that range from the extremely simple hole-and-flap variety, all the way to the extremely complicated magnetic or infrared variety that can be set to open in only, open out only, or open both ways. I recommend this magnetic door, because it keeps raccoons, dogs, and other cats out while allowing your cat in. Your cat wears a magnet on her collar that activates the door to unlock when she tries to go through. In any case, some sort of locking mechanism is recommended. This can also ensure that your cat can't go out when you don't want her to. Your choice will be based on your price range and your needs, so shop around and make an informed decision.

Q. *What eye colors are possible in cats?*

A. Eye color is genetically related to coat color.

- Pointed cats always have blue eyes.
- White cats, and cats with a lot of white markings, can have: blue eyes; green, gold, or copper eyes; or odd-eyes (one blue eye and one green or gold eye)!
- Other cats can have green, gold, or copper eyes, but not blue eyes. The most common eye colors are in the middle of the eye color spectrum (greenish-yellow to gold). The colors at the ends of the eye color spectrum (deep green or brilliant copper) are usually seen only in purebreds who have been selectively bred for extreme eye color, although they may sometimes appear in non-purebreds.

WEEK 21 CHECKLIST

✓ Learn all you can about cats. Visit websites, buy books, and talk to your vet. You'll find they are truly amazing animals (but you've probably figured that out by now).

Week 22: Surgery for Your Cat

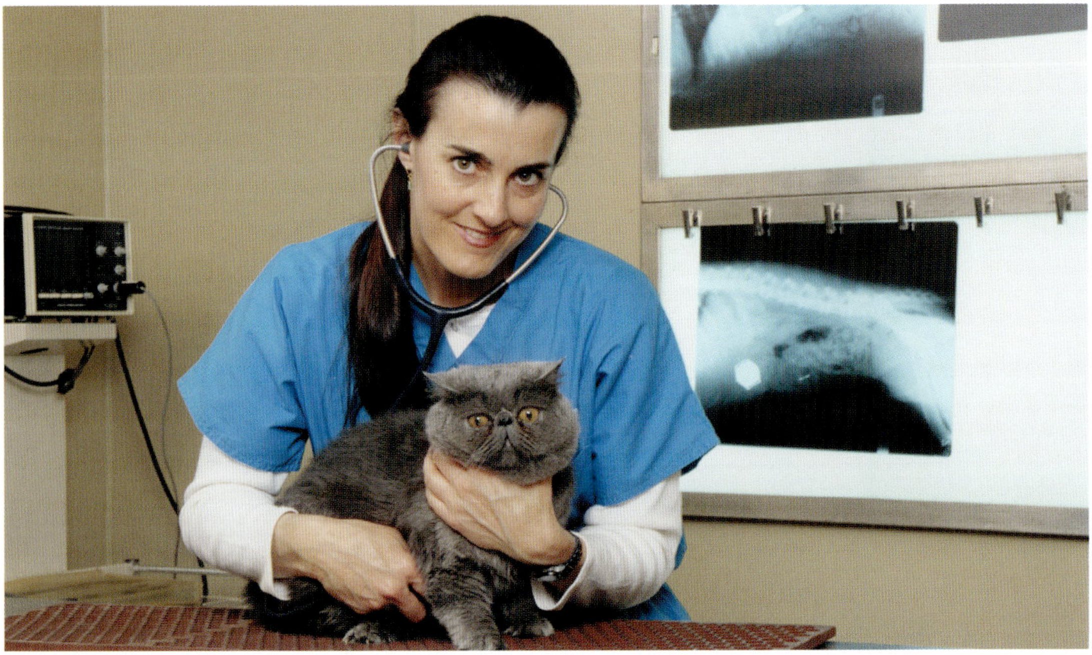

You should educate yourself on exactly what your veterinarian does in providing care for your kitten before, during, and after surgery. Issues concerning elective surgery are often not considered by the pet owner yet can be extremely serious health concerns.

Veterinarians have many options to choose from. What criteria does your vet use to select his anesthetic protocol? Is it cost, safety, ease of administration, or ability to control the depth of anesthesia? Are intravenous fluids administered during the procedure? Is any type of presurgical blood work performed? Is there any provision for pain medication and prevention? Is postoperative hospitalization included? Each of these procedures will add cost, but are all beneficial.

Too often, owners assume that because a procedure is routine there is no need for concern and the only issue to consider is price. I would simply ask one question, would you be as complacent if you were the patient being operated on? Would saving $75 or even $100 justify not taking simple precautions? Ask the questions and demand the answers.

ANESTHESIA

Generally, anesthetic agents fall into two categories: Inhalant or gas, and injectable. Injectable anesthetics

Too often, owners assume that because a procedure is routine there is no need for concern.

are generally used for short procedures such as small growth removals and diagnostic procedures. The depth of anesthesia is controlled by the dose injected. Once the dose in administered, the body has to clear the compound from the blood stream at an appropriate rate or the anesthesia may go too deep.

MEDICAL TREATMENT ISSUES AT A GLANCE

- Educate yourself on exactly what your vet does in providing care for your kitten before, during, and after surgery.
- Find out what criteria your vet uses to select his anesthetic protocol. Does he use inhalant or injectable anesthetics? Know the difference.
- Find out if IV fluids will be administered during surgery. I recommend IV fluids for almost every surgery, if for no other reason than as a safety precaution.
- Find out if presurgical bloodwork will be performed on your kitten. Don't assume that because your kitten is young that everything is normal.

If the anesthesia is too deep, the blood pressure, heart rate and blood supply to vital organs drop to dangerous levels. If this situation is not corrected quickly, tissue damage or even death could occur.

Thankfully, drug manufacturers have developed compounds that provide good anesthesia and have a reversal agent. This means that the body does not have to do all the work. There is a little chemical magic that takes place and stops the anesthesia from getting too deep. If these products are used in a general surgical procedure, then there must be someone watching the depth of anesthesia to determine when the reversal agent needs to be administered. Monitoring equipment, of various types, may be required to make the determination that the anesthesia is too deep.

Many of the same issues concerning depth of anesthesia are also concerns with inhalant anesthetics, and therefore monitoring procedures are needed. The newer anesthetic gases allow for rapid recovery because the gases are not absorbed by the body. This means that depth of anesthesia can essentially be controlled by a dial on the anesthesia machine. Again, someone must be watching as even with a dial anesthesia can get too deep.

BLOOD WORK

Presurgical blood work is a precautionary measure to help ensure that there will be no complications with the surgery. Each vet may decide what is important to check for, but taking some measures can prevent serious problems. If a patient is anemic and is placed under anesthesia, where the amount of oxygen entering the lungs is altered, then tissue damage may occur since there is already a decreased oxygen-carrying ability of the blood due to the anemia. If the protein levels are

low in the system, then the body may have trouble healing the surgical wounds normally. There are many values to check and what to check can vary depending on the individual animal. I feel it is important not to just assume that because the surgical patient is young that everything is normal. Can you imagine the outrage if a surgeon were to operate on a 3-year-old child without checking blood work for abnormalities and then there were complications? In my opinion, because I have had several cases where preanesthetic blood tests have helped identify minor problems. This is an area in which you should avoid compromise.

IV FLUIDS

Administering intravenous fluids during an anesthetic procedure is a simple method for providing safety during the procedure. Granted, most elective procedures are short enough that there will not be serious alterations in the fluid properties of the patient. However, the surgical time involved is only one factor to consider; remember than any surgery carries risks that you will want to minimize.

First, a slight degree of dehydration is likely present in each patient presented for surgery because they been off food and water for several hours prior to surgery. Secondly, most preanesthetic medications alter the way the fluid is managed in the body. Third, there is a period of time where the patient is prepared for the surgery by clipping and cleaning the surgery site. Fourth, after the surgery there is a time when the sedatives given before surgery or pain medications continue to alter the body's mechanisms.

When you consider the total time and all the circumstances, intravenous fluids are needed in almost every case. Most importantly, if there is a problem during the procedure, the first step towards stabilizing the patient is to establish an intravenous fluid line. In my opinion it is simply better patient care to be prepared for the need and have the line in and functioning than to waste time establishing the line after the need arises. Again, as with so many issues in pet care, prevention is the goal.

WEEK 22 CHECKLIST

- ✓ Talk to your vet about his procedures before, during, and after surgery.
- ✓ Research the different types of anesthesia available for your kitty.
- ✓ Make sure your vet does presurgical blood work on your kitty.
- ✓ Talk to your vet about IV fluids during surgery.

Week 23: Spaying & Neutering: The Full Story

Bob Barker ended every episode of The Price is Right with some excellent advice: "Help control the pet population! Have your animal spayed or neutered!" Unless you are planning to breed your cat, you should schedule spaying or neutering for when your pet is around six months of age. In the last few years, there has been much discussion about the pros and cons of having pets spayed or neutered even earlier. While this is technically possible, I believe this practice is best left to humane societies and other organizations whose primary focus is the reduction of pet animal overpopulation. If a responsible pet owner wants to have his animal sterilized, six months old is young enough.

SPAYING

The estrus cycle in cats is different from the cycle in dogs and humans. Unlike humans, cats do not menstruate or have a menstrual period. You will wait a long time and wind up with a lot of kittens if you wait for that event to occur in your cat. Instead, cats are *seasonally polyestrual*. This means that a cat will enter a "heat" season, and cycle

You should schedule spaying or neutering for when your pet is around six months of age.

in and out of heat once every several days until they enter their quiet season and remain out of heat for several months. How long an individual cat will remain in heat and how many cycles she will have during her season varies from individual to individual. The important thing is to recognize the symptoms your cat will display when in heat.

Heat is the time when the female cat is most receptive to the male for breeding. Her behavior will often change dramatically.

Heat is the time when the female cat is most receptive to the male for breeding. Her behavior will often change dramatically. A cat that is usually non-social may suddenly find everything and everyone extremely fun to be around. Kitty may vocalize loudly, yowling as though she is in horrible pain. She may roll around on the floor giving you the impression that something is seriously wrong, when in fact she just wants to breed... with anything!

Many owners will call emergency veterinary facilities attempting to find out what is wrong with their cat. A common test is to scratch the cat's back just above the pelvis. If there is a pronounced raising of the tail and rear, combined with a downward arching of the back (often to the point where the cat cannot stand), chances are she is in heat. Unless you're planning to breed your cat, go ahead and make an appointment with the vet to have her spayed.

The spaying operation (ovariohysterectomy) is routinely performed when a cat reaches six months of age, before she goes into heat for the first time. Generally, the procedure removes both the ovaries and all of the uterus. Abbreviated procedures may sterilize your kitten, but failing to remove the entire uterus or ovaries may cause infection or disease to develop. Talk to your vet about what procedure he will perform on your kitten.

NEUTERING

Although several veterinary organizations have tried to develop chemical sterilization techniques for male cats, neutering, or full castration, is the generally preferred and most effective method for sterilization.

In my practice, I occasionally run into male cat owners who are reluctant to have their male pets neutered. They seem to have the idea that neutering will adversely affect their cat's personality and temperament — his *maleness.* I consider a male cat owner's aversion to neutering as an inappropriate transference of his personal sensitivities.

In fact, neutering a male cat will reduce his desire to fight, reduce his desire to spray to mark his territory, and reduce the strong, offensive odor of "tomcat" urine. Those reductions alone might be adequate justification for your family to choose to neuter your pet; helping control the pet population then becomes an added benefit.

WHY SPAY OR NEUTER?

One female cat can be responsible for up to 20,000 descendants within a few years, contributing to the massive problem of overpopulation. Many people feel that it will be good for the cat to go

HORMONE-RELATED AGGRESSION

If you have an unsterilized cat, you will probably notice several behavioral difficulties.

If your cat is male you may notice that he will begin spraying areas of your home, marking his territory with a distinct, ammonia-like smell. He will also be more territorial, and more inclined to roam. The drive to find a mate is overpowering, so he may become a little aggressive if you come between him and a female in heat.

A female cat will actually go into heat at least three times a year, but possibly as often as every other week. A cat that has never shown an interest in going outdoors may suddenly be nearly impossible to keep in the house. She may yowl, rub herself along the floor, or seem to be in pain. Male cats may begin to gather near your house, sensing her condition.

These behaviors can be annoying, so if you do not have a reason to breed your cat, early sterilization is the most effective measure against these problems.

through one heat cycle or even have one litter before being sterilized, but all medical evidence points against it. There are no health benefits to waiting, and there are even a few problems that can arise from remaining "unfixed." Your cat will bear no ill effects if you spay her around four to six months. A spayed cat will be less likely to roam, and won't display any of the strange and sometimes obnoxious behaviors that go with being in heat. Consult your vet about the right time to spay your kitten.

A relatively minor surgery, neutering your cat will save you quite a few hassles later on. First and foremost, it will prevent your male cat from impregnating every in-heat female he can find, and will therefore help control the cat population. Secondly, it will control or even eliminate many of the behaviors that an intact male cat is certain to show. Among these are the tendency to roam, the habit of spraying to mark his territory, and the tendency toward aggressive, territorial behavior.

WEEK 23 CHECKLIST

✓ Educate yourself about the processes of spaying and neutering.

✓ Watch for signs of "heat" in your female cat.

✓ Take your female cat to the vet as soon as she appears to be in heat.

✓ Talk to your vet about what sterilization procedure she will use.

Kitten Development: Week 23

- Your cat is beginning to mature hormonally.
- He or she continues to grow physically.
- Although not physically full grown, a male may begin to spray to mark territory.
- A female may show signs of "heat," including loud meowing, body contortions, and a strong desire to go outside.

Week 24: Six Months & Beyond

At six months, most cats are effectively mature. Your kitten is now grown and you have done everything you can on a week-by-week basis to give your pet the best care and nurturing possible. At this point you are ready to leave the pages of this book and launch yourself and your kitty into a long healthy mature relationship.

Before you go on into the next six months of your cat's life and beyond, let me leave you with a few tips on caring for your adult cat and making the most of your bond with this wonderful and loving animal. There are lots ways you can increase your enjoyment of each other.

ADULT CAT CARE TIPS

Adjust your pet's diet

As your cat grows older his dietary needs will change. You'll want to look now at transitioning your pet off kitten food and onto an adult mix. There are a number of good brands out there, and my advice is to carefully check the nutrition label and, if in doubt, consult your vet.

Cats cannot live without protein. That is why most commercial adult cat foods are high in protein, and why your kitty will always appreciate a special treat now and then of a little tuna or a piece of cheese. Whatever you do, avoid giving your cat table scraps or food meant for any creature other than a cat.

You may want to discuss with your vet the potential for urinary tract difficulties, especially if your cat is a male. Your vet will help you decide if you should consider a cat food specially formulated to prevent these conditions. It's a good idea anyway to talk to your vet regularly about your cat's diet, and whether he or she is at risk for any other health conditions that could be mitigated or even prevented by a specially formulated cat food.

Remember, too, that older cats are less active, and their metabolic rates slow. As this happens you'll want to gradually reduce your pet's dietary protein levels and keep a close eye on her weight by reducing the amount you feed her, putting her on a weight-control formula, or both. You may also want to put down an extra water bowl to keep your cat hydrated as she grows older.

MATURE CAT TIPS

- Adjust your pet's diet from a kitten food to a mature cat food.
- Don't miss your cat's regular checkups.
- Keep your kitty well groomed at all times, including brushing and combing to reduce hairballs and mats, and keeping his nails trimmed.
- To keep your cat well hydrated as she grows older, put down an extra water bowl.
- Keep your cat comfortable as she ages by making sure she has a soft place to rest and keeping her indoors.

Don't miss those checkups

Following the theory that the best medical treatment is no treatment, keep up your cat's schedule of annual and biannual veterinary checkups, including keeping all shots and vaccinations current. Nothing is more heartbreaking than losing a pet and knowing you could have done something to prevent it. Take the time to keep your cat's wellness maintained.

When you visit your vet, have your cat's claws clipped. Ideally you should be doing this at home, but at the very least make sure your vet is doing it on a regular basis. You will need to do this less frequently as your cat ages.

Keep kitty groomed

Keeping your cat brushed will help maintain her coat and keep her skin healthy. It is also helpful in reducing hair ball production. When your kitty enters her golden years, this will become even more important, because older cats sometimes have difficulty maintaining their coats. Mats and tangles can harbor moisture and bacteria that lead to skin diseases and exacerbate any allergies your cat might have — all of which are increasingly problematic with age. You should brush your cat at least twice a week.

Keep your cat safe and comfortable

Your cat is capable of flopping anywhere and sleeping now, but as she gets older she will appreciate some soft comfortable bedding in a place protected from too much heat and cold. If your cat goes outdoors, you will probably want to keep her in more as she ages, especially during seasonal periods of intense heat or cold.

If you haven't done this already (and you should have!) make sure that, if your cat goes outside, she is wearing a name tag on her collar with your name and phone number on it. Older cats may become disoriented or lose some of the eyesight they had when they were younger, and a tag will help someone who finds your cat return your pet to you.

Play with your cat

There's not much your cat likes better than playing, unless it is playing with you. Take time out to spend some quality time with your cat each day. Playing together keeps your bond of loving friendship strong, while it keeps your cat healthy and active. Expensive toy purchases are not necessary for play. It's easy to crumple up a ball of

One of my clients keeps a supply of bubble-blowing solution on hand; her cats just love chasing bubbles around the room.

FELINE LOWER URINARY TRACT SYNDROME

Also known as FLUS, this syndrome is particularly life-threatening to male cats. Tiny crystals in the urine, the same crystals that cause kidney or bladder stones, form and can cause serious problems. These crystals irritate the lining of the urinary tract, causing an increase in the production of mucus on the lining of the urethra, the tube that carries urine from the bladder to outside the body. This can cause a serious problem in the male cat because the urethra begins with a large diameter vessel and tapers to a very small opening. When the urethra is plugged by the mucous, the cat cannot urinate.

This is condition can claim your cat's life in a couple of days. If you see your cat making frequent trips to the litter box or notice that he seems to be in pain when he tries to urinate, get to a vet right away. Delay could cause your cat to die.

Human Years versus Cat Years

Cat's Age (in Years)	Human Age Equivalent
6 months	10 years
8 months	13 years
1 year	15 years
2 years	24 years
4 years	32 years
6 years	40 years
8 years	48 years
10 years	56 years
12 years	64 years
14 years	72 years
16 years	80 years
18 years	88 years
20 years	96 years
21 years	100 years

paper, tie a feather to a string, or fill a sock with catnip and let your cat chase it around.

Lots of cats like to chase flashlight or laser pointer beams around a room and under furniture. One of my clients keeps a supply of bubble-blowing solution on hand; her cats just love chasing bubbles around the room! Just remember not to leave your cat alone with toys that have small parts or strings that she shouldn't ingest. Put those toys away when your play time is through.

BROADENING YOUR CAT'S HORIZONS

If you are a community-service-oriented person, or just have an interest in exploring more of the world together with your grown cat,

you might want to look into the possibility of enlisting in a pet therapy program, or even showing your cat.

Pet therapy

Most towns and cities have programs in which people who love animals can share the benefits of pet interaction with schoolchildren or the elderly. Typically, dogs and cats and their owners visit classrooms to help children learn more about pets and how to care for them. In some cases pets are even enlisted to help kids learn basic skills like math and reading. Pets and owners who visit nursing homes are basically there just to spread a little love and joy. I don't think I have to tell you how much it can brighten up someone's otherwise dull day to hold a sweet little kitty or puppy in their lap for an hour.

If your cat has a gregarious, laid-back personality, then he or she will probably enjoy a cat show.

If you'd like to learn more about how you and your cat can participate in pet therapy programs, contact your local humane pet shelter or rescue society.

Showing your cat

It may surprise you to learn that the first criteria you should look at if you're interested in showing your cat is not his or her outward appearance, but what the cat is like on the inside. A shy or skittish kitty is not a good candidate for a cat

CAT SHOW TIPS

- Remember that the most important issue to consider when deciding whether or not to show your cat is his temperament.
- Start exploring the show world while your cat is still young.
- Check with your vet before deciding to show your cat.
- If you got your cat from a breeder, ask him if your cat is worthy of showing.
- Check with your local cat fancier's association to get a listing of shows and information on how to get started.

show; a public event like that will only stress out your pet and be unpleasant for you as well. But if your cat has a gregarious, laid-back personality, then he or she will probably enjoy all the attention and exposure to both cats and people afforded by a cat show.

If you are interested in showing, it's a good idea to start exploring the show world while your cat is still young. Cats (like people) don't like the unexpected; as they grow older they become quite set in their ways. Even a laid-back cat can find the show scene unsettling once he has a few years on him. So start young.

You'll should also check with your vet before you go down this road. If your cat has any special health problems, it's not a good idea to expose him to the risk of infection. Cat shows take precautions to limit exposure to disease, but don't to take any unnecessary risks.

If your cat is purebred, talk to your breeder about whether she is worthy. You will be competing with cats who measure up to some high standards. But your cat doesn't have to be a full-blooded anything to compete in a cat show. Most shows have divisions for domestic cats, and there's a competition for all types of cats at all levels.

If you decide to move forward with showing your cat, contact one of the organizations in the Resources section of this book for further information. Most localities have a Cat Fancier's organization of some kind. The Governing Council of the Cat Fancy maintains a website and office with detailed listings of shows and information on how to get started in this hobby that involves many thousands of cats and owners worldwide. You never know, you just might have a champion!

WEEK 24 CHECKLIST

- ✓ Monitor your cat's weight and activity level, and make sure he is eating the correct type and amount of food.
- ✓ Be sure not to miss your cat's regular checkups with the vet.
- ✓ Keep your cat well groomed.
- ✓ Keep your cat safe and comfortable.
- ✓ Play with your cat, and give her lots of attention.
- ✓ You may want to broaden your cat's horizons by looking into pet therapy or showing her.
- ✓ Don't forget that your cat should go back to the vet at 16 months for the last fecal exam and final vaccinations (see page 54 for vaccination schedule).

Kitten Development: Week 24

- Your cat is physically mature but still acts like a kitten.
- If not yet spayed or neutered, your cat will show signs of male or female hormonal behavior.
- Your cat will continue to "fill out" as he gets older. Be sure not to let him gain too much weight.

Notes:

Notes:

Glossary

In the course of this book, I have used some medical and technical terms, as well as some words or terms that have specialized meanings, relating either to the format of the book or to raising a cat in general. In most cases, at least some basic definition or explanation is provided in the text. To help ensure that you understand these important words and terms, the following glossary is provided.

adulticide
A term referring to any flea control product that targets the adult flea rather than the eggs and larvae.

animal shelter
A facility for the care and/or disposal of stray and homeless animals. Often associated with humane societies and other animal rescue organizations, reputable shelters are committed to controlling animal overpopulation and finding loving homes for the animals in their care; such shelters are one of two highly recommended sources (along with reputable breeders) for obtaining your kitten.

antibodies
Specialized proteins that aid the immune system in fighting off infection. Kittens are born with a certain level of antibodies received from their mother, but develop their own during their first three to four months of life.

breed
As a noun, a group of animals descended from common ancestors and having similar characteristics; in other words, the kind of cat — Persian, Siamese, Maine coon.

As a verb, the mating of a male and female cat with the intent of producing kittens.

breeder
A person who breeds cats professionally. A reputable breeder will ensure that adequate prenatal and postnatal care is provided to the

mother cat and her kittens, and is one of two highly recommended sources (along with reputable animal shelters) for obtaining your kitten.

carrier
A crate designed to restrain and protect a cat during travel, for the safety of cat, owner, and other travelers; the carrier can also act as a safe place within the home.

cattery
Sometimes found in conjunction with a puppy mill (which works on the same principle), these breeding facilities breed solely for numbers, selling the animals for a profit. They are notorious for offering ill-bred animals (sometimes even inbred) and for their unsanitary conditions.

These are usually being run illegally, since many states require an individual or organization to apply for a kennel license, and to submit to routine inspections, before allowing them to keep large numbers of animals. These should be avoided as a source for a kitten because the cats they produce are subject to a wide range of defects, diseases, and other problems stemming from the environment.

conformational traits
The manner in which a cat's physical and behavioral characteristics correspond to those of its breed in general.

declawing
A surgical procedure involving the removal of a cat's claws at the last joint of the toe. Declawing is a highly controversial procedure in the veterinary community, and is usually unnecessary.

deworming
Veterinary treatment designed to clear your cat of parasites that can cause infection and illness. To completely clear your kitten, multiple deworming treatments may be necessary.

feeding trials
The preferred method of determining the nutritional benefits of a given cat food. High-quality foods will offer this information on the container, as opposed to a guaranteed analysis.

feral
Describes an animal that has not been raised in a domestic

environment. These cats usually display a fear of humans, dislike being handled, and are difficult to be affectionate with. If a kitten is adopted from the streets early enough, these traits will slowly disappear.

grooming
One of the key decision points in finding a kitten that is right for you and your lifestyle. How much your cat sheds and how much time and effort is required to maintain the appearance of its coat are issues to be considered in picking the right type of kitten for you.

guaranteed analysis
A method of nutritional analysis sometimes offered on the packaging of certain cat foods. This tells you chemically what your cat would be consuming, but not how the food will meet your cat's dietary needs.

heartworms
Infectious parasites that come from microscopic larvae carried by mosquitoes; a major threat to the health of your kitten, preventable with the use of proper medication.

heat
Common term for a female cat's estrus cycle, the period when the female will accept mating with a male; a cat in her estrus cycle is said to be "in heat," a condition characterized by a blood-tinged discharge from the vagina and certain temporary behavioral changes.

"hot spots"
Rapidly developing infection on the surface of the skin, often the result of a cat chewing its skin at the site of a bacterial infection. Preventable with proper grooming and attention.

indoor vs. outdoor
One of the key decision points in finding a kitten that is right for you and the lifestyle of your household. For the happiness of cat and owner, the important decision of whether your cat will be primarily an indoor or outdoor animal is best considered in advance.

inhalant anesthetics
One of two options for anesthetizing cats during surgery, inhalants (gases) are generally used

to keep an animal unconscious for an extended period of time during major operations.

injectable anesthetics
One of two options for anesthetizing cats during surgery, injectables are generally used for shorter operations.

intravenous fluids
Substances administered during surgical procedures to help ensure your cat's safety by maintaining its internal fluid levels.

maternal antibodies
Disease-fighting proteins that kittens receive from their mother; these provide adequate protection against infection and disease for the first several weeks of a kitten's life, but gradually lose effectiveness.

matting
Clumping of a cat's fur into tangles; usually a sign of a poor grooming routine in which a cat is not combed frequently enough. Matting is more of a problem for breeds with longer hair.

neutering
Another name for castration, the sterilization of a male cat by removal of the testicles; a highly recommended means of controlling feline overpopulation.

parasitic infection
Disease caused by harmful organisms that can invade your cat's healthy blood, tissue, and organs. Parasitic diseases are a major threat to your kitten's immediate and, if untreated, long-term health. The health effects of parasitic infections can be minimized with proper, timely testing and effective treatment. For more information on parasitic diseases, see the "Common Parasites" chart on page 59.

pediatric vaccination series
A schedule of vaccinations designed to build your kitten's immunity to disease and infection; ideally, the series begins when your kitten is six weeks old, with new vaccinations every three weeks until the kitten is between 14 and 16 weeks of age.

pet health insurance
Increasingly popular in many areas, this works just like human health

insurance, and can be a great help in dealing with unforeseen medical expenses your cat may incur.

positive reinforcement
The best way to ensure your kitten's progress in any sort of training — rewarding good behavior with food treats and lavish praise.

presurgical blood work
A highly recommended precautionary measure to help prevent unforeseen complications during surgery.

rabies
An infectious disease of the central nervous system, and one of the primary threats to animal health across the world. Vaccinating your cat against rabies protects you and your family, friends, and neighbors against the disease; in most areas, the rabies shot is the only animal vaccination required by law.

silent heat
A condition in which a female cat shows no outward sign of being "in heat," but can become pregnant.

socialization
The process by which a cat adapts or conforms to the surroundings that may affect it throughout life. This usually consists of the cat being introduced slowly to unfamiliar people, children, other cats, and possibly even other types of animals.

spaying
Sterilization of a female cat by removal of the ovaries and uterus; a highly recommended means of controlling feline overpopulation.

vaccination
An important part of your kitten's healthcare program, beginning with the pediatric vaccination series at around six weeks of age. Critical to protecting your cat from potentially life-threatening infections and diseases, including rabies.

weaning
The process by which a kitten gradually becomes accustomed to food other than its mother's milk. This will not be a concern if you get your kitten from a breeder or shelter, but inadequate weaning can be a serious issue for cat owners who are raising a newborn orphaned kitten.

Resources

About Cats
www.cats.about.com

The American Animal Hospital Association
800-883-6301
www.healthypet.com

The American Association of Feline Practitioners
aafponline.org

Alley Cat Allies
www.alleycat.org

American Cat Fanciers Association
417-725-1530
www.acfacat.com

American College of Veterinary Internal Medicine
www.acvim.org

American Pet Association
www.apapets.com

The American Veterinary Medical Association's Animal Health Page
800-248-2862
www.avma.org/care4pets

ASPCA
424 East 92nd Street
New York, NY10128
212-876-7700
www.aspca.org

ASPCA National Animal Poison Control Center
888-426-4435
800-548-2423
*Consultation fee charged. All major credit cards accepted
900-680-0000
*Consultation fee is billed to your phone number

Cats & Kittens Magazine
www.petpublishing.com/catkit/

The Cat Fanciers' Association (CFA)
732-528-9797

The Cat Fanciers' Website
*different from the Cat Fanciers' Association
www.fanciers.com

The Delta Society
www.deltasociety.org

Dumb Friends League
www.ddfl.org

Feline Advisory Bureau
www.fabcats.org

The Humane Society of the United States
National Headquarters
2100 L Street NW
Washington, DC 20037
202-452-1100
www.hsus.org

The Internet Cat Club
www.netcat.org

Natural History Museum of Los Angeles- Cats! Wild to Mild
www.lam.mus.ca.us/cats/

NetVet Veterinary Resources and the Electronic Zoo
www.avma.org/netvet

Purebred Cat Rescues by Breed
www.felinerescue.net/Purebred_Rescue_Links.htm

Spay USA
800-248-SPAY
www.spayusa.org

About the Author

Dr. Hugh Washington lives in Hoover, Alabama, a suburb of Birmingham, where he owns and operates The Met Vet, Inc. He shares operation of his practice with his wife Patti, who serves as practice manager and groomer.

Dr. Washington is a native of Decatur, Alabama, and attended Auburn University where he obtained his Bachelor of Science in Animal and Dairy Science and his Doctor of Veterinary Medicine degree in 1985.

Dr. Washington has worked in multi-doctor practices in Columbus Georgia, Huntsville, Alabama, and Birmingham, Alabama. He is a member of the American Veterinary Medical Association and has been a member of the Jefferson County Veterinary Medical Association, Mid-State Veterinary Association, The Alabama Veterinary Medical Association, and the American Animal Hospital Association. He received the 1990 Service Award from The Alabama Veterinary Association for service to the profession.

Dr. Washington was active in Rotary International and Boy Scouts during the 1990s. Also during this time he became a student at USA Martial Arts, where he continues to train and instruct. He is a member of Church of the Highlands in Birmingham, where he and his wife use their interest in cooking to help provide meals for various ministries.

Dr. Washington is the sole practitioner in his practice. His work with animals began when he was seven years old, caring for animals in his family's neighborhood. He began working in a community veterinary clinic when he was 14, and since that time has remained dedicated to his life's work, providing informed care for animals and their owners.